KU-585-047

INSTITUTE OF PSYCHIATRY

MAUDSLEY MONOGRAPHS

Number Twenty-Three

THE ROLE OF BODILY FEELINGS IN ANXIETY

By

PETER TYRER

Senior Lecturer in Psychiatry
University of Southampton
lately Medical Research Council.
Clinical Research Fellow,
Institute of Psychiatry, London

OXFORD UNIVERSITY PRESS

1975

INSTITUTE OF PSYCHIATRY

Maudsley Monographs

THE ROLE OF BODILY FEELINGS IN ANXIETY

Oxford University Press, Ely House, London W. 1

GLASGOW NEW YORK TORONTO MELBOURNE WELLINGTON
CAPE TOWN IBADAN NAIROBI DAR ES SALAAM LUSAKA ADDIS ABABA
DELHI BOMBAY DALCUTTA MADRAS KARACHI DACCA
KUALA LUMPUR SINGAPORE HONG KONG TOKYO

ISBN 0 19 712145 4

PRINTED IN GREAT BRITAIN
BY RICHARD CLAY (THE CHAUCER PRESS) LTD
BUNGAY, SUFFOLK

In memory of

M. J. T.

who understood the emotions

better than most

CONTENTS

LIST OF TABLES

LIST OF FIGURES

LIST OF FIGURES

MAUDSLEY MONOGRAPHS

HENRY MAUDSLEY, from whom this series of monographs takes its name, was the founder of The Maudsley Hospital and the most prominent English psychiatrist of his generation. The Maudsley Hospital is now united with Bethlem Royal Hospital, and its medical school, renamed the Institute of Psychiatry, has become part of the British Postgraduate Medical Federation. It is entrusted by the University of London with the duty to advance psychiatry by teaching and research.

The monograph series reports work carried out in the Institute and in the associated Hospital. Some of the monographs are directly concerned with clinical problems; others, less obviously relevant, are in scientific fields that are cultivated for the furtherance of psychiatry.

ACKNOWLEDGEMENTS

MOST of the work described in this book was carried out during the tenure of a Medical Research Council Clinical Research Fellowship and I am grateful to the Council for their support. In particular I thank Dr. Malcolm Lader, who acted as supervisor during the tenure of the Fellowship and without whose help none of the studies could have been attempted. I am especially grateful to him for allowing me to reproduce published work of which he was co-author. I also thank Professor Sir Denis Hill for acting as my sponsor and for his interest in this work. Many colleagues helped willingly in those aspects of the experiments which were required to be double-blind; they include Vivian Maclean, Drs. Alyson Bond, Monica Greenwood, and Sadru Bhanji, and their help in what was often onerous work was always galdly given. I also thank Fred Goldsmith for technical work which prevented many experiments from foundering, Barbara Kinsley for statistical advice, and Alan Brady and the staff of the Animal House at the Institute of Psychiatry for help in supplying snakes and other animals to act as phobic stimuli. I am also grateful to Malcolm Lader, Eliot Slater, and Edgar Miller for commenting critically on the manuscript, to Joan King and Audrey Pritchett for the care they took in its preparation, and to my wife, Ann, for her patience and encouragement at all stages of the work. I thank the editors and publishers of the following journals for permission to reproduce already published material:

Clinical Pharmacology and Therapeutics—FIGURES 7, 8, 10, and 11
British Journal of Clinical Pharmacology—FIGURES 4 and 19
Electroencephalography and Clinical Neurophysiology—TABLE 16
British Medical Journal—TABLE 11 and FIGURE 16
The Lancet—Part of CHAPTER X
Annals of the New York Academy of Sciences—TABLE 1

Southampton, 000 P.J.T.

INTRODUCTION

In this book a series of inquiries into the part that bodily feelings play in the genesis and maintenance of anxiety is described. There are many ways of looking at this problem and the pharmacological method chosen in these inquiries, the alteration of peripheral physiological responses using beta-adrenoceptor blockade, is only one of many. Although it has limitations the method lends itself readily to experimental study and from the data derived in differing forms of anxiety some general conclusions can be made. Because the emphasis throughout is on the role that bodily feelings play in anxiety some other aspects of the studies are not discussed at length, although they may be at least of equal importance. These include the place of beta-adrenoceptor blockade in the treatment of pathological anxiety and the merits of using physiological methods to evaluate mood change. Some of the descriptions of the techniques used have been abbreviated, particularly when they have been given in full previously in other texts, as a surfeit of such information can only bore the general reader and unnecessarily repeat what is already known to the informed one. Despite this the methods employed in the studies are given in detail because anxiety is known to fluctuate greatly in apparently similar experimental situations.

There are those who feel, like Sherrington, that 'mental events are not examinable as forms of energy and therefore lie outside Natural Science'. They regard the relevance of bodily feelings in different states of mood as a matter for the philosopher's attention rather than the scientist's. The complexities of the problem are freely admitted but this should not be an excuse for pointless speculation or despair. Whether or not the results of the studies described in the following pages are answering the questions posed by their aims is for the reader to decide, but, whatever his opinion, he must agree that the study of these phenomena cannot be the province of any one discipline. Nor can the place of bodily feelings in anxiety be regarded as a barren intellectual problem; it has an immediate relevance for all those engaged in the treatment of pathological anxiety in its many forms. Because of this I make no apology for emphasizing the psychiatric aspects of the subject at the expense of other, equally valid, approaches, in most of which morbid anxiety has seldom been considered.

CHAPTER I

RELATIONSHIP BETWEEN BODILY FEELINGS AND EMOTION: A BRIEF HISTORY

INTRODUCTION

THE changes occurring in the experience of emotion have fascinated scholars and scientists for centuries. From the beginning it was realized that certain bodily feelings accompanied emotion and their inter-relationship has provoked much speculation but little objective inquiry until recently. Aristotle stated that what differentiated the animal kingdom from plants was the presence of a 'sensitive soul'. Although this soul was not defined in detail Aristotle appeared to include both sense perception and emotional feelings under its functions He considered that only 'the male has the power of making the sensitive soul, so it is impossible for the female to generate the animal from itself alone' (*De Generatione Animalium*) Aristotle did not explain this further and also did not give much indication how sensations were related to emotion. However, his statement that 'sensation is held to be a qualitative alteration, and nothing except what has soul in it is capable of sensation' (*De Anima*) suggests that he thought sensation was a secondary phenomenon. Although the anatomical basis of the 'soul' was a controversial subject, the view that the bodily accompaniments of emotion were secondary rather than primary phenomena persisted until the 17th century. Shakespeare was aware that simulated emotion could mimic natural emotion. A player

> could force his soul to his conceit,
> that from her working, all his visage wann'd,
> tears in his eyes, distraction in's aspect,
> a broken voice, and his whole function suiting
> with forms to his conceit (*Hamlet*, Act II, Scene 2).

There is no doubt from this description that the bodily manifestations of simulated emotion were considered secondary to the 'workings of the soul'.

Descartes challenged this by his philosophy, which postulated that body (*res extensa*) and mind (*res cogitans*) were separate entities which could not be interrelated. This absolute separation has led to the term dualism being applied to the Cartesian system. Unfortunately the system is at its most suspect in its explanation of emotion (Descartes, 1648). According to Descartes, emotion was expressed in two stages. The first stage was the physiological consequences in the body following the experience of emotional stimuli ('objects which move the senses'). 'Animal spirits' passed up the sensory channels to the seat of the soul, which Descartes presumed to be the pineal

gland. A parallel change then occurs in the mind and an emotion is experienced, which may be associated with parallel bodily changes. Descartes could not allow an interaction between mind and body in his theory (hence his emphasis on parallel changes), partly because their forms were so different but also because he considered that if the mind influenced the body and vice-versa, a continuing self-generating cycle of 'movement' would be created. As the amount of 'movement' in the universe, according to his theory, was absolute and immutable, such a system would break the rules. Nevertheless, he frequently contradicts his own theory in his explanation of the origin of emotion. For example he states that—'they (emotions) may sometimes be caused by the action of the soul which determines itself to conceive of this or that object, and also simply by the temperament of the body' (*Article* LI). Thus apparently not only external objects can induce emotion but also changes of the mind and body themselves. Descartes' preoccupation with the conservation of movement allows the expression of emotions or of bodily manifestations in response to a stimulus, but not both. He described the effect of 'action of the soul' in animals, 'although they have no reason, nor perhaps any thought, all the movements of the spirit and of the gland which excites the passion in us, are none the less in them, and in them serve in maintaining and strengthening not, as in our case, the passions, but the movements of the nerves and muscles which usually accompany them. So when a dog sees a partridge he is naturally disposed to run towards it, and when he hears a gun fired, this sound naturally incites him to flight' (*Article* L). The dichotomy between mind and body is maintained, but whereas animals are bodily controlled robots humans are controlled by their souls, a rather more comfortable notion. Nevertheless, this extract shows Descartes flirting with the idea that bodily changes were the most important events in the genesis of emotion, an idea that was to lie fallow for another two hundred years.

The James-Lange Theory of Emotion

Although some of Descartes' followers, notably Malebranche (1674) re-stated the dualistic aspects of emotion, the subject essentially remained the province of philosophical inquiry until William James (1884) and C. Lange (1885) independently propounded the theory that the actual experience of emotion was secondary to perception of bodily changes. This theory galvanized psychologists and physiologists into the objective study of emotional states and their accompaniments and offered the opportunity to test their relationship scientifically. Although James and Lange are credited with the origins of this theory it will be noted that Descartes had suggested that changes occurring in the body could produce emotion (*Article* LI), although at no point did he express this as the sole cause of emotion. Charles Darwin had also touched on the same points that James used as the basis of his theory, in his treatise on the expression of emotions in both man and animals (1872). He devoted most of his attention to the description of the adaptive features of

emotion in animals and their similar counterparts in man, and in so doing adduced further evidence for his theory of evolution. In his conclusion, however, he wrote:

> the free expression by outward signs of an emotion intensifies it. On the other hand, the repression, as far as this is possible, of all outward signs softens our emotions. He who gives way to violent gestures will increase his rage; he who does not control the signs of fear will experience fear in a greater degree; and he who remains passive when overwhelmed by grief loses his best chance of recovering elasticity of mind.

While not going so far as to say that emotional experience is dependent on the perception of bodily symptoms these comments must certainly have influenced James and are virtually paraphrased in the first account of his theory (1884).

It is worthwhile considering James' theory in more detail as, although in its original form it is untenable in the light of present neurophysiological knowledge, there are some aspects which still merit careful attention. He argued his case cogently from the only evidence he had available, introspection. His hypothesis was stated clearly:

> Common sense says, we lose our fortune, are sorry and weep, we meet a bear, are frightened and run; we are insulted by a rival, are angry and strike. The hypothesis here to be defended says that this order of sequence is incorrect, that the only mental state is not immediately induced by the other, that the bodily manifestations must first be interposed between, and that the more rational statement is that we feel sorry because we cry, angry because we strike, afraid because we tremble.

He regards the whole body as 'a sounding-board, which every change of consciousness, however slight, can make reverberate', and thereby claims that even the most subtle emotional changes can be accounted for by the variation in bodily symptoms. He boldly asserts that 'emotion dissociated from all bodily feeling is inconceivable' and that objectless emotion is due to derangement of bodily functions and not mental ones. He replies to objections that deliberate inducement of bodily symptoms do not give rise to emotional states by an argument which presages the treatment currently called behaviour therapy:

> There is no more valuable precept in moral education than this: if we wish to conquer undesirable emotional tendencies in ourselves, we must assiduously, and in the first instance cold-bloodedly, go through the outward movements of those contrary dispositions which we prefer to cultivate.

Unfortunately, the most important part of James' theory is often forgotten and was certainly ignored by the physiologists who subsequently attempted to show that his hypothesis was incorrect. James himself was partly to blame for this, for in stating the main points of his theory he frequently blurred the distinction between the subjective experience of emotion and observed emotional behaviour. He added to the confusion by modifying his views in the

full account of his theory (1891). It was only in his original account that James described his theory at a neurophysiological level:

we have a scheme perfectly capable of representing the process of the emotions. An object falls on a sense-organ and is apperceived by the appropriate cortical centre; or else the latter, excited in some other way, gives rise to an idea of the same object. Quick as a flash, the reflex currents pass down through their pre-ordained channels, alter the condition of muscle, skin and viscus; and these alterations, apperceived like the original object, in as many specific portions of the cortex, combine with it in consciousness and transform it from an object-simply-apprehended into an object-emotionally-felt. No new principles have to be invoked, nothing is postulated beyond the ordinary reflex circuit, and the topical centres admitted in one shape or another by all to exist.

To disprove this theory it is necessary to show that subjective emotional feelings can occur in the absence of all bodily sensations. This is a difficult task which can only be attempted in conscious man as self-report of feelings is the only means of measurement at our disposal.

These considerations are important when it comes to evaluating the theories of emotion of currently more acceptable psychologists and physiologists. It is instructive to trace these chronologically. Lange (1885), a Danish anatomist and physician, independently arrived at the same conclusions as James, and so is usually credited as a co-originator of the theory. His own theory laid particular emphasis on the vasomotor centre as the co-ordinator of all emotional activity, and so there were substantial differences between his theory and that of James. His conclusions were not so radical. For example, his statement 'the stimulation of those cells between the brain and spinal cord is the root of the causes of the affections, however else they may be constituted: and is fundamental to the physiological phenomena which are the essential components of the affections', is an unexceptional comment that few would argue with today. Neither James nor Lange have scientific evidence for their theories and both regarded them as provocative but interesting views which needed further study.

It is perhaps surprising that the theory was accepted so readily at first. James himself did not think so; in 1890 he wrote to a friend—'it seems to me that psychology is like physics before Galileo's time—not a single elementary law yet caught a glimpse of'. The theory was accepted by psychologists rather than psychiatrists as it had theoretical rather than practical applications. Sigmund Freud in Vienna was apparently unaware of it when he described the syndrome of neurotic anxiety and its associated symptoms:

the feeling of anxiety may have linked to it a disturbance of one or more of the bodily functions—such as respiration, heart action, vasomotor innervations or glandular activity. From this combination the patient picks out in particular now one, now another, factor . . . the proportion in which these elements are mixed in an anxiety attack varies to a remarkable degree, and almost every accompanying symptom alone can constitute the attack just as well as can the anxiety itself. There are consequently rudimentary anxiety attacks and equivalents of anxiety attacks, all probably having

the same significance, which exhibit a great wealth of forms that has as yet been little appreciated (Freud, 1894).

Freud could not have avoided commenting on the James–Lange theory had he been aware of it at this time. His concept of 'anxiety equivalents' would have been seized upon by James as a perfect illustration of his theory.

The Cannon-Bard Theory

Evidence slowly accumulated over the next thirty years that the James–Lange theory was insufficient to explain many of the physiological aspects of emotion. Sherrington (1900) showed that dogs could still display emotional behaviour after complete transection of the spinal cord in the cervical region. He also severed both vagus nerves in a few animals so that only the phrenic nerve remained intact. Again a full range of emotional behaviour was shown by the animals and it seemed hardly likely that these could be secondary to peripheral diaphragmatic and cranial symptoms alone. Prideaux (1921) pointed out that there was usually a delay in the physiological response to an emotional stimulus whereas the subjective experience of emotion immediately follows perception of the stimulus. It was therefore difficult to argue that the symptoms preceded the emotional experience.

These doubts were even more strongly expressed by Dana (1921). He noted from his neurological experience that patients showed emotional behaviour and still had subjective feelings of emotion after almost complete loss of afferent and efferent stimuli. He elaborated this further and proposed the first 'central' theory of emotion. Although this was not fully comprehensive, its main tenets were identical to those of Cannon's hypothesis. As they were written six years before Cannon's thalamic theory of emotion it is surprising that Dana's contribution is not more widely known. Cannon himself freely acknowledged Dana's work in the first account of his own theory (Cannon, 1927) and it is remarkable how similar are their two hypotheses. Dana's explanation of the physiological changes in emotion are apt today:

> The centers that control the activities of the vegetative system are mainly in the brain-stem. These centers are first appealed to when the animal perceives something calling for instant action in defense, offense or active desire. They, on the other hand, stir up the muscles, viscera and glands, but they also appeal through the thalamus to the cortex and arouse the emotions appropriate to the objects recognised or idea that has been aroused (Dana, 1921).

Cannon specified that the thalamus was the central part of the emotional pathway, which, was 'released for action' by sensory stimuli or cortical impulses, led to both the experience of emotion and its bodily changes. Thalamic neurones 'not only innervate muscles and viscera but also excite afferent paths to the cortex by direct connection or by irradiation' (Cannon, 1927). Bard (1928) added further evidence that the diencephalon and associated structures were necessary for the experience of emotion when he

demonstrated that 'sham rage', induced in cats by decortication was only abolished when the postero-ventral part of the diensephalon was removed. Later work showed that Cannon and Bard were mistaken in attributing the chief role in emotion to the thalamus alone. Papez (1937) suggested that the parts of the brain collectively known as the rhinencephalon were primarily concerned with emotion rather than olfaction and the correctness of this observation has been repeatedly confirmed since. The fornix, mammillary bodies, anterior thalamic nuclei, parahippocampal, and cingulate gyri (of the brain), often known as the Papez circuit, are now collectively known as the limbic system or 'visceral brain' (MacLean, 1955), and is involved in most, if not all, emotional experience.

Cannon later delivered what many considered were the final refutations of the James–Lange theory (Cannon, 1929, 1931). He pointed out that bodily symptoms experienced in acute emotion could be explained as the by-product of sympathetic nervous discharge and that they could also be produced by the exogenous administration of adrenaline. The sympathetic division of the autonomic nervous system was activated at times of 'flight or fight' and the cranial and sacral division (parasympathetic division) were responsible for 'building up reserves and fortifying the body against times of stress'. Thus the symptoms of emotion were explicable as adaptive features; it was of great benefit to the fleeing animal pursued by a predator to have an increased muscle blood flow and a quicker reaction time, and the subjective symptoms experienced by the animal were only a reflection of the internal physiological changes induced by sympathetic nervous and humoral discharge.

Current Theories of Emotion

There have been many other theories of emotion since Cannon's. These can be loosely grouped into psychological and physiological ones. The former include Brown and Farber's theory of frustration (1951) and motivational theories of emotion (Leeper, 1948; Webb, 1948), which were developed more fully by behaviour theorists (Mowrer, 1950; Miller, 1951). In these theories the emphasis is laid on the external stimulus and overt response aspects of the emotion. By contrast, the physiological theories concentrate on the internal aspects and neglect the external concomitants. These include Freeman's homeostatic theory (1948) in which emotion is considered as a result of imbalance between cortical, unlearned, and conditioned stimuli, Arnold's excitatory theory (1950), in which the autonomic symptoms of emotion are attributed a similar role to that in the James–Lange theory, and are considered necessary to convert 'emotional attitude' to 'emotional expression', and Hebb's central theory (1946b), which ignores stimulus-response patterns entirely, laying emphasis on the central neuronal changes which ultimately must lie at the heart of all cerebral functioning.

It is not proposed to discuss these in detail; most are speculative and based on limited evidence, and furthermore, have virtually no predictive value.

Those that are based to some extent on known aspects of the physiology of the nervous system emphasise one aspect at the expense of another and tend to over-simplify a complex series of processes. There are two theories which do not fall into this category and which have been shown to be heuristically useful. Both are based primarily on experimental evidence.

The first, which has become known as the activation theory of emotion, was propounded by Lindsley in 1951 (though it should be noted that Duffy's theories had antedated this). He based this on the evidence of a series of experiments carried out by him and his colleagues during the previous three years. The best known of these was the demonstration that an 'activated' electroencephalogram similar to that of acute emotional excitement could be produced in an anaesthetized animal by stimulation of the brain-stem reticular formation (Moruzzi and Magoun, 1949). Acute injury to the ascending neuronal pathways from the reticular formation—later dubbed the ascending reticular activation system (ARAS)—prevented this pattern of activation following stimulation (Lindsley, Bowden, and Magoun, 1949), and chronic lesions of the ascending pathways in cats produced emotional apathy and somnolence (Lindsley, Schreiner, Knowles, and Magoun, 1950). Lindsley therefore proposed that the reticular formation, which has anatomical connections with the hypothalamus and medullary centres responsible for autonomic outflow, served as an 'EEG activation mechanism' which aroused the cortex under suitable stimulus conditions, and, simultaneously, activated the lower brain-stem centres responsible for the expression of bodily symptoms. Lindsley later showed that this theory provided an explanation for the different psychological phenomena associated with the electroencephalogram. He suggested a behavioural continuum, ranging from deep sleep, associated with slow frequency high voltage (delta) waves, to extreme arousal or excitement, associated with high frequency, low voltage, asynchronous (beta) waves in the electroencephalogram (Lindsley, 1952). This valuable concept was immediately seized by psychologists and psychophysiologists as it provided an explanation for much of the apparent inadequacies of physiological measurements as predictors of emotion. Several workers (e.g. Malmo, 1959; Duffy, 1962) have emphasized that both autonomic and central physiological measures are indicative of an 'arousal state' rather than of a specific emotion. The concept explained why, for example, physiological measures were so remarkably similar in different emotional states; the state of arousal was the same, and it was from this crude substrate that the subtlety of the emotion was fashioned. It became clear that understanding of the genesis of specific emotions would not be achieved by physiological measures alone. Although the arousal concept has been recently criticized for its failure to explain, for example, the generally poor correlations found between different autonomic measures in arousal states (Lacey, 1967) it remains too valuable to be discarded.

The second hypothesis developed from the classical work of Schachter

and Singer (1962). They showed that the experience of subjective emotion was highly susceptible to cognitive factors. Their method of investigation is often quoted because of its novelty and also, I suspect, because unlike most such descriptions it makes highly entertaining reading. They injected naïve subjects with either adrenaline or saline, informing half of them what symptoms to expect and keeping the rest in ignorance, and then subjected them to different experimental situations. Two groups were placed in a situation conducive to euphoria by introducing a stooge who joked and ridiculed the whole experiment. He actively encouraged the experimental subjects to participate in this tomfoolery. The other two groups were exposed to another stooge who criticized and complained about the tasks set in the experiment, encouraging the subjects to do the same. At the end of the experiment the subjects rated themselves and were objectively assessed for each of the major emotional states. Not surprisingly, those in the first group rated themselves primarily as happy or amused, while those in the second group were antagonistic and angry. The important finding was that those subjects who were ignorant of the effects of adrenaline rated themselves as more amused or more angry than those who knew what symptoms to expect. Thus, in the author's words, 'given a state of physiological arousal for which an individual has no immediate explanation, he will "label" this state and describe his feelings in terms of the cognitions available to him' (Schachter and Singer, 1962). This conclusion neatly combined psychological and physiological aspects of emotional states and provided a more satisfactory explanation of the genesis of emotional states than other theories. The importance of cognitive factors was stressed adequately for the first time, and showed the dangers of oversimplifying emotional experience.

Later workers have laid more stress on the complexity and difficulty in interpreting emotional states. Bindra (1969) illustrates the caution of current opinion in this subject by emphasizing that perceived emotions can result from a wide variety of external and internal stimuli, and so it would be unreasonable to expect a simple one-to-one relationship between emotional experience and bodily reactions. Other investigators have concentrated on the cognitive factors in emotional experience, showing how powerful they can be in influencing the perception of pain (Nisbett and Schachter, 1966) and anxiety (Valins and Ray, 1967). Valins' work is of particular interest as he has shown how important can be the effects of heart rate in inducing or relieving emotion. By giving false heart-rate feedback to subjects in different experimental situations he and his colleagues have effectively shaped emotional response, heightening emotion by increasing feedback rate and lowering emotion by reducing it (Valins, 1970). This reminds us that, whatever the complexities of emotional experience, it is unwise to dismiss its autonomic correlates as entirely secondary phenomena.

Although the bodily changes taking place in normal emotion have been relegated to a minor position by the recent emphasis on cognitive factors they

have been considered to be more important in pathological emotion. The postulate of a cycle of emotion leading to bodily changes and thus reinforcing further emotion, which Descartes considered to be the logical consequence of close relationship between body and mind, has been reintroduced. Richter (1940) suggested that in pathological anxiety 'emotional discharge may in itself be sufficient to cause a further release of adrenaline through the action of the sympathetic nervous system: the original coenaesthetic impulses are increased and a vicious circle may result'. Breggin (1964), in a review of the relationship between adrenaline and anxiety also suggested that positive feedback could be operative in reinforcing anxiety. 'The acute anxiety reaction can become self-generating, since the symptoms of the anxiety reaction can reinforce the reaction, causing it to spiral. Similarly, each separate anxiety reaction can further condition the individual to respond in the future to his own internal cues with more intense anxiety reactions.' These mechanisms can only operate in the setting of pre-existing anxiety and therefore leave the chief question, of how the abnormal anxiety is caused in the first place, unanswered. Nevertheless this work suggests that a combined approach, in which both normal and abnormal emotion are studied, might be of value. Unfortunately, a Cartesian-like dichotomy between psychologist and psychiatrist in the study of emotion has existed for many years. It has stultified the development of both disciplines and led to too much pointless theorising on the one hand, and an excess of narrow-minded empiricism on the other. In the studies described in succeeding chapters these dangers have been appreciated. If they have not been entirely avoided I nevertheless hope that the reader's conclusions will not be the same as those of William James eighty years ago:

> As far as 'scientific psychology' of the emotions goes, I may have been too surfeited by too much reading of classic works of the subject, but I should as lief read verbal descriptions of the shapes of rocks on a New Hampshire Farm as toil through them again. They give one nowhere a central point of view, or a deductive or generative principle. They distinguish and refine and specify in infinition without ever getting on to another logical level (James, 1891).

CHAPTER II

BETA-ADRENOCEPTOR BLOCKADE AND ITS RELEVANCE TO THE STUDY OF EMOTION

Introduction

THE chief purpose of this review is to establish a rationale for the experimental work that follows. It is not intended to be an exhaustive account of the pharmacological aspects of beta-blockade or of the psychological significance of catecholamines in emotional states. The association of the disciplines of pharmacology, physiology, psychology, and psychiatry is a somewhat unusual one and it is necessary to sketch the scenario before proceeding with the play. An account of the development of the beta-adrenoceptor blocking drugs follows and the relevance of these agents in the study of normal and morbid emotion is discussed.

SECTION I

Historical Aspects of Adrenergic Blockade

The concept of adrenergic receptor blockade merits description in some detail, because without it the pharmacological actions of adrenergic blocking drugs (sympatholytics) are difficult to interpret. It has been known for many years that stimulation of sympathetic nerves or the external administration of sympathomimetic agents produces different effects on different organ systems. Langley (1905) was the first to suggest that 'receptive substances' were present in the tissues and that the action of chemical and nervous stimuli was dependent on the relative proportion of such substances in the tissues. Soon afterwards Dale (1906) noted during the pharmacological evaluation of the ergot alkaloids that ergot blocked the pressor effects of adrenaline but not its cardiac ones. He followed this up by studying the effects of ergot on a wide range of effector organs, and was able to separate these into three groups, a predominantly inhibitor group, a predominantly motor (excitatory) group and a mixed group containing both elements. He had in fact separated the alpha-effector organs from the beta-effector ones, as ergot was subsequently shown to be an alpha-adrenoceptor blocking drug. Unfortunately this work went relatively unnoticed although pharmacologists continued to be made aware of the differential response in adrenergic effector organs. It was shown that the inhibitory effect of ergotamine on uterine smooth muscle could be reversed by raising the concentration of adrenaline sufficiently (Gaddum, 1926). This was the first demonstration that adrenergic blocking agents acted by com-

petitive inhibition. The concept of adrenergic receptors was thus further refined; in Gaddum's words, 'there is an area in the muscle on which the adrenaline must act and (that) a fraction of this area is blocked by ergotamine so that in any given case the concentration of adrenaline must be increased in a certain proportion to produce the same effect'. Although ephedrine was soon shown to have similar inhibitory properties (Curtis, 1929; Finkleman, 1930) the confusion produced by the original description of excitatory and inhibitory effects of adrenaline prevented further elaboration of receptor theory. Instead it was proposed that the reason for the variation in adrenergic response might be the presence of two different transmitters at nerve endings, Sympathin I and E (Cannon and Rosenblueth, 1937).

It was not until 1948 that the confusion was resolved. Ahlquist studied the effects of five different sympathomimetic amines on a variety of effector organs and showed that there were two rank orders of potency, one headed by adrenaline, concerned mainly with vasoconstriction and smooth muscle contraction, and the other headed by isoprenaline and concerned mainly with vasodilatation and cardiac excitation (Ahlquist, 1948). Adrenaline has since been shown to possess the characteristics of both groups and noradrenaline is a more appropriate example. Ahlquist named the receptors concerned with the first group, alpha receptors, and those with the second group, beta receptors. In so doing he satisfactorily explained the differential effects of sympathetic stimulation without recourse to terms which implied a mode of action. In general, the excitatory effects of adrenaline are mediated through alpha-receptors and inhibitory ones through beta-receptors, the most important exception being the cardiac effects. The types of receptor in the different adrenergic effector organs are shown in TABLE I.

Although later work has supported Ahlquist's classification it is worth emphasizing that the concept of different adrenergic receptors remains very much a theory. Ahlquist himself has pointed out that we are still no nearer to demonstrating the existence of such receptors than we were twenty years ago (Ahlquist, 1967). It was the pharmacological isolation of the first beta-adrenoceptor blocking drug, dichloroisoprenaline (Powell and Slater, 1958), that led gradually to the acceptance of Ahlquist's classification, although at the time the authors did not fully appreciate the significance of their discovery. The synthesis of further beta-adrenoceptor blocking drugs leading to the introduction of pronethalol (nethalide) into clinical practice (Dornhorst and Robinson, 1962), preceded a plethora of clinical and pharmacological studies of the actions of beta-adrenoceptor blocking agents that shows no sign of abating. By contrast, studies of alpha-adrenergic blockade have been fewer, and although there are many alpha-adrenoceptor blocking drugs available they have in the main been used as pharmacological tools rather than clinical agents. It is for this reason that they have been excluded from study in this thesis. There is no reason why they should deserve any less investigation than

TABLE 1 CLASSIFICATION OF ADRENERGIC EFFECTOR ORGANS
(adapted from Nickerson (1967) and Moran (1967)

EFFECTOR ORGAN	RESPONSE TO STIMULATION	RECEPTOR TYPE
Arteries	Vasoconstriction	alpha
Arteries	Vasodilation	beta
Heart—sino-auricular node	Increased frequency of firing	beta
Heart—atrio-ventricular node	Increased frequency of firing	beta
Heart—ventricle	Increased force of contraction	beta
Bronchial muscle	Relaxation	beta
Gastro-intestinal sphincters	Contraction	alpha
Urethral sphincters	Contraction	alpha
Uterus	Contraction (usually)	alpha
Stomach	Relaxation	alpha and beta
Intestine	Relaxation	alpha and beta
Radial muscle of iris	Contraction	alpha
Ciliary muscle	Relaxation	beta
Submaxillary gland	Secretion	alpha

N.B. Metabolic effects are not included as it is doubtful whether these are true alpha or beta effects

beta-adrenergic blocking agents, particularly in the study of emotion, but until recently there were no safe agents available without unwanted effects in clinical dosage. Now that new compounds satisfying this criterion have been introduced (e.g. indoramin) (Royds, Coltart and Lockhart, 1972); their effects in emotional states deserve inquiry.

Pharmacology of Beta-Adrenoceptor Blockade

An adrenergic effector organ is presumed to have specific beta-receptors when (i) there is a characteristic action to a given beta-agonist or group of beta-agonists, and (ii) the tissue response produced by the agonists can be prevented by a specific beta-antagonist (Dollery, Paterson, and Conolly, 1969). These antagonists should not affect response to other pharmacological agents acting through different receptors or by direct action on the tissue. All known beta-adrenergic blocking drugs act by competitive antagonism (Fitzgerald, 1969; Dollery, Paterson, and Conolly, 1969) so that it is possible to overcome the effect of the beta-antagonist by raising the dose of agonist sufficiently. The dose-response curve is moved to the right with each increment of antagonist but the shape of the curve and maximum response are unaltered. The presence of competitive antagonism often creates difficulty in making comparison between different beta-adrenergic blocking agents and emphasizes the value of flexible dosage in clinical studies.

The actual changes which occur when an agonist or antagonist encounters the beta-receptor are open to speculation. The terms 'affinity' and 'intrinsic activity' have been introduced to explain one part of the process (Ariens, van Rossum, and Simonis, 1959). An antagonist or agonist has a high affinity if it readily combines with the receptors, but its pharmacological effects are dependent on the intrinsic activity of the 'drug-receptor complex'. High intrinsic activity is shown by agonists and low intrinsic activity by antagonists. It is not clear whether the 'drug-receptor complex' is produced by replacement of receptor by the drug (Clark, 1933) or by an actual reaction between drug and receptor (Paton, 1961) and until it is possible to measure these changes at a cellular level the prospect of resolving this is remote. Some clues have come from a study of structure-activity relationships of beta-adrenergic agonists and antagonists. It must surely be relevant to receptor theory that almost all beta-adrenergic blocking drugs are very similar in structure to isoprenaline, a potent beta-agonist (Ariëns, 1967) [FIG.1], and that the stereo-isomers of these drugs show such differences in their beta-blocking properties (Belleau, 1967).

Although the group of drugs classified as beta-adrenergic blocking agents for fundamentally similar in that their chief action is one of beta-receptor antagonism, there are differences in their other pharmacological effects. These include 'intrinsic sympathomimetic activity' and 'membrane activity'. Intrinsic sympathomimetic activity is the presence of sympathomimetic effects—despite adequate blockade of beta-receptors to other beta-agonists (Dollery *et al.* 1969). Thus the 'drug receptor complex' has beta-agonist properties as well as antagonist ones. Because the agonist activity is intrinsic it becomes manifest even though the same activity would be antagonized if it came from an external source. Intrinsic agonist activity is often sufficient to limit the clinical value of a beta-adrenoceptor blocking agent; it prevented the first of the group to be discovered, dichloroisoprenaline, from being used in normal practice (Moran and Perkins, 1958). The effect may also be a problem if sympathetic stimulation should be kept at a minimum (e.g. thyrotoxicosis) (Turner, 1971). The term 'membrane activity' includes both local anaesthetic and quinidine-like properties and as these show important physiological differences from quinidine itself (Vaughan Williams, 1966) it is preferable to use an alternative term. Although Fitzgerald (1969) has classified beta-adrenergic blocking agents on the basis of these additional effects it is doubtful whether this is of much practical value. Apart from a few exceptions these additional pharmacological properties are of little clinical significance and even those effects which were first thought to be due to local anaesthetic activity (e.g. suppression of ectopic beats) have been shown to be beta-adrenergic blocking effects (Coltart, Gibson, and Shand, 1971).

Central Effects of Beta-Adrenergic Blocking Drugs

This subject has been deliberately excluded from the discussion of the pharmacological aspects of beta-blockade because the central effects reported are almost certainly independent of beta-adrenergic blocking action. Certainly, it is impossible to relate central effects to peripheral beta-blockade in any way whatsoever. In some ways this is surprising. Recent work has shown that noradrenaline and other nonoamines are intimately concerned with cerebral neuro-transmission (Fuxe, Dahlström, and Hillarp, 1965; Hillarp, Fuxe, and Dahlström, 1966). Only a small proportion of the total noradrenaline is available for interaction with drugs and other substances, the remainder being tightly bound in core vesicles in nerve fibres (Axelrod, 1965). The proportion that is available is affected by both alpha and beta-adrenergic blocking drugs in peripheral nerves; both groups reduce the release of noradrenaline and inhibit noradrenaline uptake in sympathetic nerve granules (von Euler, 1966). As both groups of adrenergic blocking drugs have similar actions the Ahlquist classification is of no help, and many other types of receptor have been postulated. The same confusion exists in the interpretation of the metabolic effects of beta-blocking drugs. The most important of these effects is an increase in plasma concentration of free fatty acids (Pilkington, Lowe, Robinson, and Titterington, 1962). Blocking of the hyperglycaemic response to adrenaline also occurs in some species, but only with certain beta-blocking drugs (Hunninghake, Azarnoff and Waxman, 1967). Several authors have pointed out that adenosine 3,5-phosphate (cyclic AMP) is involved in these effects and speculate whether a common factor links them (Moran, 1967; Robison, Butcher, and Sutherland, 1967). It has also been postulated that some of the central and metabolic effects of beta-blocking agents could be explained by the existence of a 'dopaminergic' receptor. Dopamine is considered to be the prototype dopaminergic agent, and this has only weak alpha-adrenergic and beta-adrenergic activity. Such an hypothesis predicts the central actions of adrenergic blocking drugs better than the Ahlquist one (Van Rossum, 1966).

It is not surprising that study of the central actions of these drugs adds little to our knowledge of the fundamental mechanisms involved. Pronethalol, in an early study, was shown to reduce spinal reflexes by a mechanism independent of its local anaesthetic action (Morales-Aguilera and Vaughan Williams, 1965). Leszkovsky and Tardos (1965) showed that propranolol in very large doses (100 mg/kg) produced narcosis in mice, and in lower doses (20 mg/kg) produced ataxia. They also showed that propranolol in smaller doses (6–14 mg/kg) had anticonvulsant properties. By contrast, another beta-blocking agent, INPEA, does not possess these properties and may have a central stimulant action (Murmann, Almirante, and Saccani-Guelfi, 1966). Pronethalol and propranolol have been shown to promote avoidance learning (Merlo and Izquierdo, 1971) and to have tranquillizing properties (Bainbridge

and Greenwood, 1971) in rats. Central muscle relaxant properties have also been described (Sinha, Srimal, Jaju, and Bhargava, 1967).

Central effects in man have been reported fairly frequently but the total numbers have been small. For example, Stephen (1966) reported only forty-seven instances of putative symptoms of central origin in 1500 patients treated with propranolol. The most frequently reported symptom was light-headedness. One symptom which does occur in a minority of patients and which is unlikely to be due to peripheral effects is that of visual hallucinations. This has been reported by several authors (Gillam and Pritchard, 1965; Stephen, 1966; Hinshelwood, 1969; Zacharias, Cowen, Presst, Vickers, and Wall, 1972). In almost all instances the daily dosage at the time the unwanted effects were experienced was at the upper end of the therapeutic range. Even moderately high dosage produced surprisingly few unwanted effects of any sort. In one study, a single dose of 120 mg of racemic propranolol at night produced no demonstrable change in the sleep pattern of normal subjects, and no withdrawal symptoms were shown. By contrast debrisoquine and guanethidine, two commonly used anti-hypertensive drugs, interfered with sleep significantly (Dunleavy, MacLean, and Oswald, 1971). Oxprenolol also has no measurable central effects after single doses of 40 mg and 80 mg by mouth and intravenous injection. (0·1–0·2 mg/kg body weight) (Turner and Hedges, 1973). There has only been one reported study in which evidence of central action has been found at moderate dosage (Bryan, Efiong, Stewart-Jones, and Turner, 1974). Propranolol was found to produce significantly slowing of reaction time after 80 mg by mouth, suggesting a central depressant action in this dosage, but the slow reaction time could have been a peripheral effect and so should not be regarded as crucial evidence.

To summarize, central effects are produced by beta-adrenergic blocking drugs in high dosage but the evidence is equivocal; with normal therapeutic doses central effects appear to be independent of beta-adrenoceptor blocking activity and there are great differences between different drugs in the type and degree of the central effects shown. In man, unwanted, apparently central, effects occur in a small minority of patients treated with large doses, but the incidence of these is only about 2–3 per cent of the total treated.

Clinical Applications of Beta-Adrenergic Blocking Drugs in Medicine

Cardiac disease

From the pharmacological effects summarized in Table 1, most of the clinical applications of beta-adrenoceptor blocking drugs can be deduced. By far the most important group of conditions in which these drugs have been proved to be useful is that of cardiovascular disorders. This subject has been widely reviewed (Fitzgerald, 1969; Dollery, Paterson, and Conolly, 1969; Harrison, 1972) and it is outside the scope of this work to describe it in any detail. Angina pectoris, cardiac arrhythmias, hypertension, and obstructive

cardiomyopathies are all significantly improved by treatment with beta-blocking drugs provided that sympathetic stimulation is contributing to the condition. If sympathetic activity is essential to maintain normal function (e.g. complete heart block, incipient cardiac failure) then beta-adrenoceptor blockade is potentially harmful. It is important to emphasize that in all these conditions the therapeutic action is a consequence of beta-blockade. For this reason there is very little difference between the therapeutic actions of different beta-adrenergic blocking drugs, provided that they are given in equipotent dosage (Thadani, Sharma, Meeran, Majid, Whitaker, and Taylor, 1973).

Thyrotoxicosis

There have been a number of reports showing that the symptoms of thyrotoxicosis are improved by beta-blockade (Hadden, Montgomery, Shanks, and Weaver, 1968; Howitt and Rowlands, 1966; Shanks, Hadden, Lowe, McDevitt, and Montgomery, 1969; Turner, 1971). These symptoms are similar to those of increased sympathetic activity, but are not necessarily a consequence of increased activity. Sensitivity to sympathetic stimulation is increased in thyrotoxicosis (Rosenblum, Hahn, and Levine, 1933) and it is possible that this alone is sufficient to account for thyrotoxic symptoms. For this reason beta-adrenoceptor blocking agents with little or no intrinsic sympathomimetic activity are preferred in treating thyrotoxicosis (Turner, 1971). Treatment of thyrotoxicosis or thyrotoxic crisis (Parsons and Jewitt, 1967) by beta-blockade is no substitute for the correction of the underlying disorder with antithyroid drugs, surgery or radio-iodine therapy. Beta-adrenoceptor blockade is probably most appropriate before surgical treatment, where it compares favourably with other preoperative procedures (Michie, Hamer-Hodges, Pegg, Orr, and Bewsher, 1974).

Tremor

Beta-adrenergic blockade has been claimed to be effective in many conditions in which tremor is a prominent symptom. These include thyrotoxicosis, Parkinsonism (Herring, 1964; Owen and Marsden, 1965; Strang, 1965; Vas, 1966), and essential tremor (Murray, 1972; Gilligan, Veale, and Wodak, 1972; Pakkenberg, 1972). Apart from their established use in thyrotoxicosis, beta-adrenergic blocking drugs are not yet widely used in these conditions.

Marsden and his co-workers have shown in an ingenious series of experiments that tremor due to increased secretion of catecholamines is reduced by beta-blockade and that the mechanism of action is probably a peripheral one. Physiological tremor is increased by adrenaline, and this increase is blocked by racemic propranolol but not by d-propranolol (Marsden, Foley, Owen, and McAllister, 1967). Similar results were found when tremor was increased by the endogenous liberation of adrenaline provoked by hypoglycaemia in Parkinsonian patients, but emotional increase in tremor produced by the stress of mental arithmetic was not attenuated by propranolol (Marsden and

Owen, 1967). A later investigation, in which intravenous racemic propranolol was given to patients with thyrotoxicosis and presumed anxiety states (i.e. patients with suspected thyrotoxicosis who were euthyroid), showed that tremor was reduced in both groups to a significantly greater extent than by a saline injection (Marsden, Gimlette, McAllister, Owen, and Miller, 1968).

There is thus good evidence that types of tremor due to an increase of sympathetic activity are appreciably reduced by beta-blockade. The clinical relevance of this is still not certain. Suggestions that tremor might be reduced by a central action of beta-blockade (Vaughan Williams, 1967) are speculative and a peripheral action is the more likely.

Migraine

It was noted in two studies in which propranol was used to treat angina pectoris that coexisting migraine was appreciably helped (Wykes, 1968; Bekes, Matos, Rausch, and Torök, 1968). There have been conflicting reports since; both negative (Sjaastad and Stensrud, 1972) and positive effects of beta-adrenergic blockade (Weber and Reinmuth, 1972) have been claimed in the treatment of this condition. From a theoretical viewpoint it is possible to postulate a mechanism of action if beta-blockade is effective in migraine. Vasodilatation of arteries is mediated through beta-receptors [Table 1] and beta-blockade may relieve the symptoms of migraine through vasoconstriction. At present the evidence for a beneficial effect in migraine is slender and the subject needs fuller inquiry.

SECTION 2

The Relevance of Beta-Blockade in the Context of Anxiety

There have been over two thousand articles published on the clinical aspects of beta-adrenergic blockade and it would be impracticable to discuss these in detail. There have been even more publications on the clinical features and treatment of anxiety. The two subjects interleave in only one area; activation of the sympathetic nervous system occurs in anxiety and beta-adrenergic blockade modifies the bodily response to this activation. Whether or not this pharmacological effect is of value in the treatment of morbid anxiety is difficult to determine. Fitzgerald (1969) has rightly pointed out the questions that a clinician ought to ask when considering treatment with a beta-blocking agent, 'Is there evidence, in this patient, of inappropriate sympathetic activity and is this contributing significantly to the patient's condition?' Certainly many patients with anxiety have inappropriate sympathetic activity but the extent to which this contributes to the condition is quite a different matter.

Sympathetic Activity in Anxiety

There is now abundant evidence that the sympathetic system is overactive in anxiety and in many other emotional states characterized by high arousal.

Until recently much of this evidence was indirect and based largely on studies in which sympathomimetic substances were administered both to anxious and normal subjects. The first of these studies set the pattern for much of the later work. Wearn and Sturgis (1919); and Tompkins, Sturgis, and Wearn (1919) administered intramuscular adrenaline (now considered a dangerous procedure) to normal controls and to army recruits suffering from the 'irritable heart' syndrome, a condition probably synonymous with anxiety neurosis, in which fatigue, dizziness, and cardiovascular symptoms (palpitations, faintness, missed beats, etc.) were prominent. They noted that normal subjects showed an increase in pulse rate and were aware of their tachycardia, but few other effects were noted. By contrast, the neurotic patients not only experienced a change in bodily symptoms but also noted subjective changes characteristic of anxiety, in some cases as acute attacks of panic. Most of the later studies produced similar results. Marañon (1924) differentiated between the effects of adrenaline in non-anxious and anxious subjects. In the former, the physiological changes produced by an injection of adrenaline were either noted in isolation or accompanied by

> une sensation émotive indéfinie, mais perçue 'en froid', sans émotion proprement dite;

in the latter, the subjective feelings were more pronounced.

> comme une émotion involuntaire, complète, c'est-à-dire avec les mêmes éléments somatiques que dans le cas précédent, et en plus la participation psychique affective qui est le complément de ces éléments.

The differences in the results of later workers could be explained in retrospect by the presence or absence of anxiety-provoking environmental cues. In a neutral setting the injection of adrenaline produced no emotional changes or 'cold emotion' (Cantril and Hunt, 1932; Richter, 1940; Basowitz, Korchin, Oken, Goldstein, and Gussack, 1956; Frankenhauser, Järpe, and Matell, 1961; Pollin and Goldin, 1961). In an anxiety-provoking setting, intentionally or unintentionally created by the experimenters, subjects showed more evidence of anxiety and in a minority of cases panic attacks were elicited (Lindemann and Finesinger, 1938; Dynes and Tod, 1940; Richter, 1940). Patients with pre-existing neurotic anxiety were more prone to these changes than normal subjects.

Recent work has confirmed that catecholamine excretion is increased in states of high arousal. Before 1954 this evidence was only circumstantial, derived from studies in which exogenous catecholamines were given. In 1954, however, von Euler and Lundberg demonstrated an increase in urinary catecholamine excretion in aircrew and passengers during flight and suggested this was due to increased anxiety. Similar results have now been shown in a wide range of stress situations, including psychiatric interviews (Elmadjian, Hope, and Lamson, 1957), examinations (Bogdonoff, Harlan, Estes,

and Kirshner, 1959) motor-car driving (Smith and Bennet, 1958; Taggart, Gibbons, and Somerville, 1969), before hospital admission (Tolson, Mason, Sachar, Hamburg, Handlon, and Fishman, 1965), and before dental treatment (Edmondson, Roscoe, and Vickers, 1972). In these situations the increased arousal is usually shown as anxiety, but the actual nature of the affect produced is not important; similarly high carecholamine excretion has been observed after seeing a highly amusing film (Levi, 1965). Psychiatric patients, in whom the stressors are more difficult to define, also have higher catecholamine excretion rates than normal controls (Regan and Reilly, 1958; Sulkowitch and Altschule, 1959; Nilsson, 1960).

There is therefore general agreement that in almost all forms of stress there is increased catecholamine production and excretion. This agreement does not persist when it comes to deciding the relative significance of different catecholamines in these changes. Noradrenaline and adrenaline production are both increased during stressful procedures, adrenaline through direct stimulation of the adrenal medulla, and noradrenaline mainly through sympathetic nervous discharge (von Euler, 1946). Most workers are agreed that increased adrenaline production can occur solely because of altered mood, but there is doubt about the cause of the changes in noradrenaline production. Several studies have shown that in active subjects under stress and in anger there is increased noradrenaline excretion and higher plasma noradrenaline levels (Elmadjian, Hope, and Lamson, 1957; Silverman, Cohen, Shmavonian, and Kirshner, 1961; Martin, 1961; Taggart and Carruthers, 1972). The apparent psychophysiological distinction between anxiety and anger is also considered to be due to differences in the secretion of adrenaline and noradrenaline (Ax, 1953; Funkenstein, 1955). Many other workers have failed to confirm these findings and they cannot be taken as proven. One explanation may be that in anger there is more muscular activity, and as this alone may raise noradrenaline levels (von Euler and Hellner, 1952) it could account for these differences.

Beta-Adrenergic Blockade and Emotional States

From the above evidence it can be seen why anxiety appears to be the most appropriate emotional state to study the effects of beta-adrenergic blockade. Adrenaline, a catecholamine with both alpha and beta-agonist properties, is secreted in greater amounts in all forms of anxiety, and noradrenaline, which is primarily an alpha-agonist, plays little or no part. In most other emotional states, the role of catecholamines is more complex and quite different from that in anxiety (Schildkraut, 1965); in depression the role of catecholamines is more speculative, and the difficulties associated with the study of anger are mentioned above.

A full account of clinical studies of beta-adrenergic blockade in anxiety follows in Section 3. At this point it is worth emphasizing that studies of the pharmacological effects of beta-blockade in anxiety and stress only form one

part of the picture; these changes have to be related to the subjective experience of anxiety if they are to be of any value. Anxiety as a symptom may show itself in innumerable ways, many of them through bodily channels. Selective blocking of these channels is not important unless the source of the anxiety is also affected. To take a simple analogy, it would be foolish to assume by plugging the outflow from a bath that water has ceased to flow into it. True, an observer standing outside notes that water no longer enters the drain, but he would be silly to infer from this that the tap had been turned off.

SECTION 3

Beta-Adrenergic Blocking Drugs in Psychiatry

There has been relatively little interest in the possible psychiatric indications for treatment with beta-blockade until fairly recently. The results of the earliest clinical studies suggested that at least some of the patients who were helped by treatment with beta-blockade could be considered as having subjective rather than physical complaints. Two cardiac conditions which were described before the introduction of beta-adrenergic blocking drugs into clinical practice, vasoregulatory asthenia (Holmgren, Jonsson, Levander, Linderholm, Sjöstrand, and Ström, 1957) and hyperkinetic heart syndrome (Gorlin, 1962), include most of the functional cardiac disorders in which beta-adrenergic blockade is useful. The chief characteristics of these conditions are an increased cardiac output with supraventricular tachycardia and labile hypertension. In the hyperkinetic heart syndrome these symptoms may interfere sufficiently with cardiac function to produce cardiac failure.

Unfortunately, these terms have not proved sufficient to describe the conditions found by other workers. An abundance of names describes what appears to be the same condition. These include 'hyperdynamic beta-adrenergic circulatory state' (Frohlich, Dunstan, and Page, 1966), 'nervous heart complaint' (Nordenfelt, Persson, and Redfors, 1968), 'hyperventilation syndrome' (Suzman, 1968, 1971), 'neurocirculatory asthenia' (Marsden, 1971), and the 'hyperkinetic heart syndrome' (Bollinger, Gander, Pylkkänen, and Forster, 1966). The authors of all these papers have found beta-adrenergic blockade to be helpful in the treatment of their particular condition. Similar benefit has been claimed in other functional cardiac disorders by Besterman and Friedlander (1965), Gault (1966) and Schweitzer, Pivonka and Gregorova (1968).

After reading these reports it becomes clear why so many of these conditions have been described as though they were separate entities. There are two parts to each condition, a disorder of cardiac function with appropriate symptoms and signs, and a diffuse mixture of symptoms which is due to anxiety. The latter include palpitations dyspnoea, dizziness, weakness and lassitude, lability of mood, and hyperventilation. Relative preponderance of

one or more of these symptoms accounts for the variation in the adjectives used to describe these disorders.

In all these syndromes treatment with beta-adrenergic blocking drugs results in a fall in pulse rate and cardiac output, stabilization of the blood pressure and often a relief of symptoms. Turner, Granville-Grossman, and Smart (1965) showed that these changes could occur in anxious patients treated with a single dose of propranolol and cardiac disorder need not be present for them to occur. Similar changes had been shown in anxious patients treated with a single dose of intravenous propranolol (Harris, 1965) and in induced fear and anger in normal subjects (Harris, Schoenfeld, Gwynne, Weissler, and Warren, 1964). No attempt was made to assess subjective changes in mood in any of these studies.

This work was the stimulus which led to the first psychiatric study of beta-adrenergic blocking drugs (Granville-Grossman and Turner, 1966). This study is worth describing in some detail because it has often been misquoted since. They used a simple cross-over design in which anxious outpatients took racemic propranolol 20 mg four times daily, and placebo for one week each. Order effects were allowed for by randomising the allocation of the first treatment. The number of patients entering the trial was determined by a closed sequential design using drug preference as the index of efficacy, and the trial terminated when a boundary was crossed (Armitage, 1960).

After each patient had completed both treatments the assessing psychiatrist indicated a preference for the more effective of the two. After fifteen patients had completed treatment the assessor's preference showed that propranolol was significantly preferred to placebo. Detailed analysis of the results, however, showed that only autonomically mediated symptoms were significantly improved on propranolol; anxiety, tension, and other symptoms showed some improvement but this was not significant. This fact has often been forgotten by later workers who have stated that the trial proved that propranolol was an effective anti-anxiety drug.

Although this work was received with interest it was not further developed. There were no other controlled trials of beta-adrenergic blocking drugs in psychiatric conditions until 1969, although Suzman (1968) had suggested from his experience with propranolol in cardiac patients that primarily anxious patients could benefit from treatment. In a single-blind trial forty patients with somatic symptoms primarily attributed to anxiety were greatly helped with propranolol. As many of these patients relapsed on placebo the author concluded that propranolol was responsible for their initial improvement.

Wheatley (1969) reported a trial of propranolol versus chlordiazepoxide in the treatment of patients in general practice with anxiety. 105 patients were treated by thirty-five general practitioners and no significant differences were found between the two drugs on overall assessment, although chlordiazepoxide was significantly more effective in relieving depression and sleep

disturbance. It is difficult to draw many conclusions from this study. Anxiety states in general practice tend to improve in the absence of specific treatment and this may obscure effects due to drugs. As no placebo control was included the relative proportion of the total improvement due to drug action could not be determined.

More recently, Bonn, Turner, and Hicks (1972) carried out another trial using a sequential design, in which the new cardioselective beta-adrenergic blocking drug, practolol, was compared with placebo. The assessing psychiatrist again chose the better of the two treatments after each patient had taken practolol and placebo for two weeks each in fixed dosage. A dramatic difference was shown between the two treatments; all fifteen patients in the trial improved more on practolol than placebo according to the assessing psychiatrist. It had been previously shown that the dextro-rotatory isomer of propranolol had no beneficial effect in anxious patients (Bonn and Turner, 1971). As this drug has only $\frac{1}{60}$th of the beta-blocking activity of the racemic mixture (Howe and Shanks, 1966), it was concluded that propranolol exerted its beneficial action by peripheral beta-blockade. As practolol does not penetrate the brain in any appreciable quantity (Scales and Cosgrove, 1970), the results of the trial reinforced the view that central action was unlikely to be responsible for the improvement.

Beta-blocking drugs have also been used to elucidate the mechanisms of lactate-induced anxiety. Lactate infusions have been shown to induce anxiety in susceptible subjects (Pitts and McClure, 1967) and this might be due to adrenergic stimulation. It has clearly been shown that beta-receptors are not involved as propranolol has no effect on the subjective symptoms experienced after lactate infusion and does not prevent the concurrent tachycardia (Arbab, Bonn, and Hicks, 1971).

There have been other reports of benefit with beta-blockade in acute anxiety in the last two years. None of these has been a controlled study and so the findings should be treated with some reservation. Earlier studies had suggested that acute anxiety in normal subjects was relatively unaffected by beta-blockade, despite clear-cut evidence of a reduction in somatic effects. Anxiety experienced in simulated aircraft flight (Eliasch, Lager, Norrbäck, Rosen, and Scott, 1967), during stressful mental arithmetic (Holmberg, Levi, Mathe, Rosen, and Scott, 1967) and under hypnosis (Cleghorn, Peterfry, Pinter, and Pattee, 1970) is not affected by propranolol in acute dosage. Recent reports suggest that 'examination nerves' are particularly helped by propranolol in small doses (Conway, 1971; Brewer, 1972), and that oxprenolol reduced subjective anxiety before public speaking (Somerville, Taggart, and Carruthers, 1973). These claims require substantiation. It must be mentioned that although adequate pharmacological blockade is easily achieved in stressful situations with a consequent reduction in pulse rate and free fatty acid levels, plasma catecholamine levels are not affected (Taggart and Carruthers, 1972). There is still no evidence that sympathetic *activation* is reduced by beta-

blockade in stress, and so it is not surprising that the subjective experience of anxiety is little affected.

There are other psychiatric conditions in which beta-adrenergic blocking agents have been used in therapy. Carlsson and Haggendal (1967) showed that haemodynamic and subjective changes characteristic of acute anxiety occurred after withdrawal of alcohol from addicted patients, and later, in a double-blind trial, propranolol was shown to be significantly more effective than placebo in relieving tension and depression (Carlsson and Johansson, 1971). Although the authors of this paper speculate that this improvement might be due to a central effect, they used propranolol in only moderate dosage (40 mg q.d.s.) and gave no evidence to support a central action. Similar improvement in the long-term treatment of an alcoholic patient with propranolol was clearly related to a reduction in somatic symptoms (Tyrer, 1972).

Heroin addiction has also been treated with propranolol and it has been claimed that this exerts a general calming and anti-craving effect which could be of prophylactic value (Grosz, 1972). In the treatment of acute psychotic states propranolol has been given in large dosage (1000–2400 mg daily) and striking benefit has been claimed within 48 hours of starting treatment (Atsmon, Blum, Wijsenbeek, Maoz, Steiner, and Ziegelman, 1971). Similar improvement is said to occur in puerperal psychoses (Steiner, Latz, Blum, Atsmon, and Wijsenbeek, 1973). These investigations were uncontrolled and the findings need confirmation.

Apart from these latter conditions, most clinical experience with beta-adrenoceptor blocking drugs has been in the field of anxiety, presenting as a primary or secondary condition. On balance the evidence suggests that any beneficial action possessed by these drugs follows their peripheral actions rather than central ones. Whether these are sufficient to ascribe an anti-anxiety action is not yet definite, but the evidence is strong enough to merit close attention, not only because of possible practical benefit, but also to re-examine the relationship between psychic events and somatic events in anxiety.

CHAPTER III

AIMS

THE chief purpose of the studies described in later chapters was to use a pharmacological mechanism, beta-adrenoceptor blockade, to answer the following questions:

(i) are beta-adrenoceptor blocking drugs suitable agents for investigating the relationship between experience and peripheral bodily changes in anxiety?
(ii) are bodily feelings important in the genesis and maintenance of anxiety?

Lange stated in his monograph (1885) that 'no man is capable of differentiating between psychical and somatic feelings. Whoever attributes a sensation to the mind, does so only on basis of theory, not on basis of immediate perception.' Methods are however now available for measuring the physiological effects of anxiety and other emotions in the body, and if it is possible to separate central and peripheral components of emotion the difficulty noted by all from Descartes onwards in judging the source of emotion can be overcome. William James spoke of 'reflex currents' between brain and viscera but gave no evidence to support their existence; we now know what these nervous pathways are and have a safe way of reversibly blocking their transmission of nervous (and humoral) effects at a peripheral level. So it appears that we can selectively do in man what Sherrington could do only crudely in dogs, to detach the 'emotional pathways' of the peripheral nervous system from the hypothalamus and higher centres and measure any changes in emotional feeling as well as observed behaviour.

Before this relationship could be investigated directly it was important to exclude coincidental central nervous system effects of beta-blockade, as these, if present, would contaminate the results and make firm conclusions impossible. The first priority was therefore to establish whether central effects could be detected with beta-adrenoceptor blocking drugs in normal dosage. If central effects were present in low dosage these agents would be unsuitable for further inquiry. This question was therefore examined in the first experiment.

Throughout the discussion in previous chapters the beta-adrenergic blocking drugs have been referred to in general terms. Although these drugs share the properties of beta-blockade there are other differences between them; it was important to select the most appropriate agents for study in these experi-

CHAPTER III

ARMS

ments and use them throughout. The two drugs chosen were propranolol and sotalol. Propranolol was selected because it is the most commonly used beta-adrenergic blocking agent; in fact it is the only one available in the United States. It has no intrinsic sympathomimetic activity, an important advantage from the point of view of its subjective somatic effects. Sotalol (MJ 1999) was therefore studied as well, for this is the only beta-adrenergic blocking drug

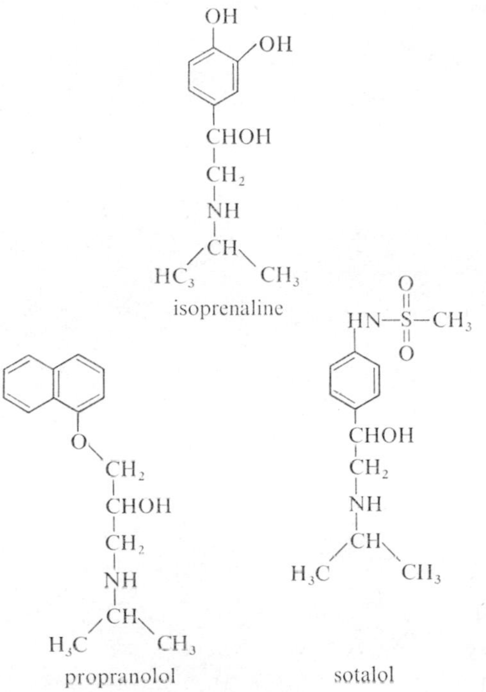

isoprenaline

propranolol

sotalol

Figure 1

with no intrinsic sympathomimetic or membrane activity (Fitzgerald, 1969). The close structural relationship between these two drugs and the beta-agonist, isoprenaline, is shown in FIGURE 1.

The assessment of the effects of these drugs in the experiments was three-pronged; psychological, physiological, and pharmacological measurements were all made. The detailed description of these follows in CHAPTER IV but it is helpful to explain at this stage why the particular measures used were chosen.

PSYCHOLOGICAL MEASURES

Despite the many advances in psychophysiology in the past few years, the measures that are available essentially measure the state of arousal of the subject. No matter how sophisticated and how many measures we use, in the last resort we have to ask the subject how he is feeling before we can have any firm notion of the emotional effects of our experimental procedure (Lader,

1969; Aitken and Zealley, 1970). It is therefore necessary to include rating scales of one sort or another so that the subjective experience of emotion is measured in our inquiries. In addition, clinical rating scales, completed by the assessing doctor, are important in studies with psychiatric patients. These are no substitute for the patient's own subjective assessment of his symptoms, however, and so both were included in the clinical trials. There are many different rating scales used in psychology and psychiatry, and criticisms can be levelled at all of them. In general, however, the use of visual analogue scales has been shown in practice to be more sensitive than interval or categorical scales, particularly in assessing changes in mood within subjects (Aitken, 1969; Little and McPhail, 1973). The term 'visual analogue scales' (VAS) is a little pretentious for a procedure which merely involves placing marks on lines but it has become generally accepted. These scales were used for both subjective and observer ratings of mood and associated symptoms in all the studies to be described, not only because of their proved value in recording variation in mood, but also because they are so much quicker to complete than other scales.

In addition to psychological assessment of mood it is often useful to know whether any drug has an effect on performance. This is particularly important for a drug which might have central nervous system effects and so these measures were used primarily in the first experiment. Fortunately a wide range of measures was available for the assessment of performance as this had been used in other experiments to determine the hangover effects of different hypnotic drugs (Walters and Lader, 1971; Bond and Lader, 1972; Bond, 1972; Bond and Lader, 1973). These measures are described in Chapter IV.

Physiological Measures

The choice of physiological measures in these studies was determined chiefly by the known pharmacological effects of beta-blockade. At the same time it was felt that undue concentration of effort on the cardiovascular effects of these drugs would be unwise. The effects of these drugs on the cardiovascular system have already been studied in minute detail and it would be pointless to duplicate these using measures which were far less complex than those available to most clinical pharmacologists. As anxiety involves changes in many other autonomic and somatic symptoms it was felt to be more profitable to look at these as well. The only true central psychophysiological measure, the electroencephalogram, was also included as without it measurement of central effects would have been incomplete.

Pharmacological Measures

It has been shown that there are wide variations in response to an individual beta-adrenergic blocking drug even when it is given in equal doses (mg/kg) (Paterson, Conolly, Dollery, Hayes, and Cooper, 1970). This explains why very large doses are used in some patients if clinical response is not achieved

in moderate dosage (Prichard and Gillam, 1969). Although some of these differences may be due to variation in sympathetic tone, a more important cause of inter-subject variation is the difference in rate of metabolism of the drug. Propranolol, which has a half-life of 2 hours (Fitzgerald and Scales, 1968), may show many-fold differences in plasma levels in different subjects after a single dose (Coltart and Shand, 1970).

It was therefore decided to include plasma estimations of propranolol in addition to the other measures. As there is some evidence that the maximum plasma level after a single dose occurs at the same time as maximum beta-blockade (Paterson *et al.*, 1970), the estimation of plasma level was of added value. This does not mean that plasma level necessarily correlates highly with beta-blockade. Propranolol has two main metabolites, 4-hydroxy-propranolol and naphthoxylactic acid (Bond, 1967), and there is now evidence that 4-hydroxy-propranolol has beta-blocking activity itself (Paterson, *et al.*, 1970). Much higher plasma levels of propranolol are needed to achieve the same degree of beta-blockade after intravenous than after oral administration (Coltart and Shand, 1970), and this difference is probably due to the presence of an active metabolite following hydroxylation in the liver, after oral administration only.

Sequence of Investigations

In the sequence of investigations described in the following chapters the emphasis has been placed on the relationship between bodily feelings and anxiety. As anxiety covers a wide range of mood states and can be both normal and pathological the studies were designed to encompass as many as possible of these variations. There were many other points of interest raised by the results of these studies, not the least of which is the place of beta-adrenoceptor blocking agents, if any, in the treatment of pathological anxiety. Much less space is devoted to these as they are incidental to the main subject. Fuller attention has been given to such questions elsewhere (Lader and Tyrer, 1972; Tyrer and Lader, 1973; Tyrer and Lader, 1974 a,b,c). In the final chapter a synthesis of the findings is given and the theoretical and practical implications described.

CHAPTER IV

GENERAL METHODS

BECAUSE of the considerations discussed in the last chapter many methods were used to assess the effects of beta-blocking drugs. The techniques used for each measure were identical in each experiment and for this reason they are described fully in this chapter and only referred to briefly elsewhere. Only one of the measurements used in these studies was original (the bodily symptom scale) and because of this the techniques are described relatively briefly.

It would have been impossible to measure the many physiological variables in the experiments simultaneously without the use of on-line computer facilities. Using a small laboratory computer (PDP 12A model—Digital Equipment Corporation Limited) skin conductance, reaction time, the components of the auditory evoked response and wave-band analysis of the electroencephalogram were all measured simultaneously. Finger tremor and power spectral analysis of the electroencephalogram were also measured on-line. Dr Malcolm Lader kindly made available the complex machine-language programs he had written for the analysis of these measures.

As bodily feelings in anxiety were being assessed it was important to measure those bodily changes which might be related to somatic symptoms. Because of this, the peripheral physiological measures chosen were those which manifest themselves at a conscious level during stress. Sweating, tremor, palpitations, and tachycardia, difficulty in breathing and muscular tension are all noted in anxiety and complained of by patients. The most appropriate physiological measure for each of these states was chosen for recording. One exception was the electromyogram (EMG). This has been shown to be related to subjective symptoms of muscular tension in anxious patients (Sainsbury and Gibson, 1954), and might have been included in these investigations. One other psychophysiological measure which was not included but which has been shown to be a useful index of arousal is forearm blood flow (Kelly, 1966). As this has no subjective concomitants it was not considered. Finger tremor, skin conductance, pulse rate, and respiratory rate were all recorded in the course of the succeeding experiments. One advantage of these four peripheral measures chosen is that they are all concerned with different physiological systems. As beta-adrenergic blocking drugs only block a few adrenergic effector organs it is helpful to have measures of other organ systems which are not affected by beta-blockade directly.

Throughout these studies stress was laid on the relationship between subjective feelings and the objective measurement of the physiological changes subserving these feelings. This chapter therefore discusses the methods of recording these at a subjective level and describes the other measures of psychological function and performance, and this is followed by an account of the physiological measures. These are deliberately described under the headings of the bodily feelings with which they are most closely related. The two purely central physiological measures are described at the end.

SUBJECTIVE AND CLINICAL RATINGS

Subjective Assessment of Mood

For these experiments a rating scale had to satisfy several criteria. All such scales have to be reliable and valid indices of what they purport to measure (Kreitman, 1961; Foulds, 1965), and in addition, for these studies it was necessary to have a measure which was sensitive to small changes in mood, particularly to changes induced by drugs. It was important to use a measure which was not influenced by extraneous factors irrelevant to the experimental situation. These include personality variables and complex mood changes occurring as a result of intra-psychic events.

It was for this reason that analogue scales were chosen as the chief instrument of self-rating. These scales have been popularized in this country by Joyce (1968) and Aitken (1969), who discuss their advantages in some detail. The most persuasive argument in their favour is the empirical one; they have been shown to work. As a general rule, categorical scales are more sensitive the more categories they contain. An analogue scale with no anchor points can be regarded as having any number of categories depending on the accuracy of scoring. It can be regarded either as a non-parametric or a parametric measure and so either form of statistical analysis can be used with the data. The scales are particularly useful for comparing ratings of mood on several occasions within the same subject. Comparisons between subjects are rather less valuable because of variations in the mental 'set' of different individuals. Some persistently score at the extreme end of the scales; other deviate little from the middle range.

The scale chosen for the subjective assessment of mood was one which originally derives from an adjective check list (Nowlis and Nowlis, 1956). Such check-lists have been used frequently in psycho-pharmacological experiments and have been shown to be useful. The subject is required to denote which of the adjectives most accurately describe his mood. Unfortunately the response he makes is necessarily an 'all-or-nothing' response; he cannot grade it in any way. Norris (1971) has taken some of these adjectives and incorporated them into a set of 16 linear scales. These were used in the present series of experiments and are shown in Figure 2. Norris grouped the

scales into different categories on a common sense basis; this has not been confirmed by principal component analysis of ratings from 500 normal subjects (Bond and Lader, 1974). In their analysis three factors were extracted; a general factor of cerebral functioning, including the psychological states of attention, vigilance, wakefulness, and efficiency, a second factor of contentedness and a third of calmness. In FIGURE 2 these three factors, the general (G), pleasure (P), and anti-anxiety (A) factors are appended to the scales and their main loadings given.

RATINGS OF BODILY FEELINGS

As subjective interpretation of bodily feelings was thought to be an important variable in the assessment of the psychological effects of beta-adrenergic blockade, it was felt essential to include a measure of these feelings. There has been surprisingly little work carried out on this subject, possibly because interest in rating scales and questionnaires developed after the James–Lange theory was discredited, and since then bodily symptoms have seldom been considered separately from mood states. More recently there has been a resurgence of interest in autonomic or 'bio-feedback' but attention in this work is primarily concentrated on the subjective effects of changing feedback rather than the actual experience of the symptoms themselves.

Mandler and his colleagues (Mandler, Mandler, and Uviller, 1958; Mandler and Kremen, 1958) have attempted to measure bodily feelings and to correlate this with objective measurements of autonomic activity. In the absence of other scales they constructed an autonomic perception questionnaire (APQ), consisting of thirty graphic (equivalent to linear) scales, seventy items from the Minnesota Multiphasic Personality Inventory (Hathaway and Meehl, 1951), and free response descriptions of autonomic symptoms. A shortened form called the body perception scale (BPS) was also used. This comprised twenty items from the MMPI and fourteen items from the Taylor Manifest Anxiety Scale (Taylor, 1953) referring to somatic symptoms. None of these scales were thought to be satisfactory for the purposes of the proposed studies; they took a long time to complete and too many questions failed to distinguish between 'state' and 'trait' feelings. For example, one of the Taylor scale items included in Mandler's scale is that statement 'I have a great deal of stomach trouble.' This does not specify what kind of stomach trouble, whether it applies over a long period or just at the time of questioning, and fails to take account of individuals with gastrointestinal diseases which may be quite independent of mental state.

Because of this a short rating scale comprising eight lines of 10 cm each was constructed to cover the chief bodily feelings experienced at a conscious level in anxiety. The feelings chosen described functions which were physiologically independent. The scale, illustrated in FIGURE 3, is easy to understand and takes a very short time to complete. No problems were encountered with it in practice.

AGE: ____________ SEX M:F DATE: ____________ TIME: ____________

1. Please rate the way you feel in terms of the dimensions given below
2. Regard the line as representing the full range of each dimension
3. Rate your feelings as they are at the moment
4. Mark clearly and perpendicularly across each line

			Factor	Main loading
ALERT	____________	DROWSY	G	0·83
CALM	____________	EXCITED	A	0·85
STRONG	____________	FEEBLE	G	0·62
MUZZY	____________	CLEAR HEADED	G	0·76
WELL CO-ORDINATED	____________	CLUMSY	G	0·64
LETHARGIC	____________	ENERGETIC	G	0·78
CONTENTED	____________	DISCONTENTED	P	0·68
TROUBLED	____________	TRANQUIL	P	0·70
MENTALLY SLOW	____________	QUICK WITTED	G	0·64
TENSE	____________	RELAXED	A	0·68
ATTENTIVE	____________	DREAMY	G	0·79
INCOMPETENT	____________	PROFICIENT	G	0·59
HAPPY	____________	SAD	P	0·82
ANTAGONISTIC	____________	AMICABLE	P	0·74
INTERESTED	____________	BORED	G	0·61
WITHDRAWN	____________	GREGARIOUS	P	0·59

G = general factor P = pleasure factor A = anxiety factor

Figure 2

CLINICAL RATING SCALES

Many rating scales are used for the assessment of clinical anxiety; these have been described in detail elsewhere (Aitken and Zealley, 1970; Lader and Marks, 1971). The one chosen for these studies was the Hamilton Anxiety Scale (Hamilton, 1959), which has been widely used in research practice. The scale has been modified so that scores could be made on analogue scales (Lader and Marks, 1971). One advantage of the scale for the purposes of these

Below there are a number of symptoms concerned with bodily changes. Please rate the way you feel for each of them at the moment. Each line represents the full range for each symptom. Mark clearly and perpendicularly across each line.

	absent	very severe
Sweating	______________________________	
Shaking or trembling	______________________________	
Palpitations or heart beating fast	______________________________	
Feelings of sickness or nausea	______________________________	
Looseness of bowels	______________________________	
Need to pass water frequently	______________________________	
Difficulty in breathing normally	______________________________	
Muscular tension	______________________________	

Figure 3

studies is that it clearly differentiates between somatic and psychic symptoms of anxiety. This has been confirmed by factor analysis of ratings (Hamilton, 1959, 1969). The scale was easy to use in practice, although it did give rise to some problems of interpretation which are discussed in CHAPTER VI.

The Hamilton Anxiety scale was completed at each clinical assessment. The scale took approximately 20 minutes to complete and in view of the many other forms of assessment it was thought to be unwise to include any other clinical assessment apart from one of overall improvement. Although this is often considered a crude measure, it is the most sensitive to treatment effects in most published studies (Kellner, 1972). This was one of the reasons why a sequential form of analysis was chosen in the first clinical trial [CHAPTER VI], although again there were difficulties in the interpretation of the results which could not have been anticipated at the outset.

PSYCHOLOGICAL TESTS

Most of these tests were carried out in the first experiment to determine whether beta-adrenergic blocking agents had any central effects. A wide range of these tests was chosen to cover the many aspects of motor and cognitive function.

Reaction Time

The subject was seated in a padded chair behind which was placed a loudspeaker. Thirty-two standardized click stimuli of moderate intensity were administered through the loudspeaker at random intervals 8–12 seconds apart. The experiment was run on-line to the computer, which controlled the timing between successive clicks. The subject's right hand was resting over a morse key, and he was asked to press the key as quickly as possible as soon as each click was heard. The reaction time in milliseconds was recorded by the computer. The reciprocal of each reaction time was calculated to give a measure of speed and the average of the thirty-two scores computed. The subject was unaware of his individual reaction times during the experiment.

Tapping

Tapping a key as quickly as possible over a specified time period is a convenient and simple measure of motor efficiency. The technique used was similar to that used in other experiments (Dickins, Lader, and Steinberg, 1965; Walters and Lader, 1971). The subject was asked to press the key as many times as possible in 60 seconds, this period being timed with a stopwatch. The subject was requested to press the key with the same finger (or fingers) throughout this time, and not to change his strategy of tapping as there is some evidence that subjects adopt different techniques of key tapping even over a short a period as 60 seconds and this may contaminate the results (Frith, 1967).

Card-Sorting

This is also a commonly used measure in psychological experiments as the type of card-sort can be altered so that both cognitive and motor elements are tested (Berry, Gelder, and Summerfield, 1965). In the experiment to detect central effects thirty-two cards were used. These were divided into four groups of eight cards, each group having one, two, three, or four spots on each card. The subject was timed while he carried out four sorts. In the first and last of these the subject was timed while he sorted the thirty-two cards into four compartments; each compartment was marked with one, two, three, or four dots and the cards had to be sorted into the appropriate categories. The average of these times was taken as the 'cognitive sort'. On the second and third occasions the cards were handed to the subject face down so that he was presented with blank cards. He was asked to sort these into four equal piles as

quickly as possible and timed over this period. The average of these two times was taken as the 'motor sort'.

Digit Symbol Substitution Test (DSST)

This test is a sub-test of the Wechsler Adult Intelligence Scale (WAIS) (Wechsler, 1958) and is a good measure of new learning ability. The test includes motor and cognitive components but the latter predominate. It has been used previously as a test in psychopharmacological experiments (Kornetsky, Vates, and Kessler, 1959). One of its chief snags is that practice effects can be quite pronounced, and because of this different versions of the test were used at each time of testing. Despite this, significant practice effects did occur (see Chapter V).

The subject was timed for ninety seconds while he coded series of symbols into boxed squares. The number correctly completed in the time was recorded. The detailed instructions were given from the WAIS manual.

Symbol Copying Test (SCT)

This test was devised by Kornetsky *et al.* (1959) as a strictly motor test. Similar symbols are used as for the DSST but the subject was not asked to code these. Instead, he copied as many symbols as possible in ninety seconds. Again, because of practice effects different versions of the test were used each time but this did not prevent significant order effects occurring.

Complex Reaction Time Test

A more difficult test measuring visual reaction time was used. A triangular black box, on which was mounted five coloured lights, was placed in front of the subject. He was instructed to press the appropriate key at the base of each light whenever the latter lit up. The experiment was run on-line to the computer. On each occasion 100 trials were run, each light was lit up for 1 second and there was a 1-second interval between successive trials. The order of illumination of the lights was random. The reciprocal of the reaction time was calculated and the mean for the total 100 trials stored on tape.

PERIPHERAL MEASURES

1. Sweating

Sweating is increased in anxiety and emotional excitement, and the measurement of the changes that occur and their relationship to emotion has long been of interest to psychophysiologists. The literature on this subject is so large that it is not proposed to discuss it in any detail. It is sufficient to note that most investigators have found that changes in the galvanic skin response (GSR), spontaneous fluctuations in skin resistance and skin conductance—the most commonly used measure, to be significantly different in anxious and normal subjects (Solomon and Fentress, 1934; Malmo, Shagass, Davis,

Cleghorn, Graham, and Goodman, 1948; Howe, 1958; Lader and Wing, 1966). There has been argument about which derivation is most appropriate in physiological experiments and to justify the ones used in this series of investigations it is necessary to review the evidence.

Sweating has a thermoregulatory function in poikilothermal animals but not in man and other homiotherms, in whom the possession of a temperature regulating system in the brain-stem prevents them from being 'shackled by thermodynamic fetters' (Tunnicliffe, 1961). At high environmental temperatures, however, there is increased sweating, particularly from the palms and soles (Wilcott, 1963). Care must be taken to allow for this fact in interpreting the results of some experiments. Most palmar sweating at normal temperatures is emotionally determined (Kuno, 1956) and so most psychophysiological experiments measure the changes in sweating in this area. Paradoxically, sweating is controlled by a cholinergic mechanism (Dale and Feldberg, 1934) and the psychogalvanic reflex as measured by change in electrical resistance is also cholinergic (Lader and Montagu, 1962). Methods used to measure sweating can be divided into two groups, those which measure skin resistance under uniform conditions, including raw resistance and conductance (the reciprocal of resistance) and mathematical derivations from these such as root or logarithmic transformations; and those which measure change in resistance, either to a defined stimulus (psychogalvanic reflex (PGR), galvanic skin response (GSR)), or in the absence of such stimuli (spontaneous fluctuations in skin resistance).

Measures used in these studies

(i) *Log skin conductance.* Skin conductance correlates highly with quantity of sweat secreted (Darrow, 1934). As in most experiments the distribution of skin conductance is skewed a logarithmic transformation is indicated (Lacey and Seigel, 1949), particularly if parametric statistics are to be used in analysis.

(ii) *Variability in skin conductance.* This was not a measure which was expected to reveal much information, but was included as both induced anxiety in normal subjects and anxiety in patients may occur in acute form (panic attacks). If these were interspersed with periods of relative calm the variance in the total record would be much greater than in less anxious subjects. In fact no patient or normal subject did have such an attack during recording.

(iii) *Habituation in skin conductance.* When normal subjects and anxious patients are exposed to a succession of identical stimuli the patients show less habituation than the normal subjects (Howe, 1958; Lader and Wing, 1966). The measure is more sensitive than raw or log skin conductance in differentiating between normal controls and patients. The regression over the period of recording was calculated and included in the print-out of results on each

occasion. Habituation in normal subjects can be marked and must be taken into account in evaluating the results of serial studies (Duffy and Lacey, 1946).

(iv) *Spontaneous fluctuations.* Since the first report that spontaneous fluctuations in skin conductance were useful indicators of level of anxiety and other forms of high arousal (Lacey and Lacey, 1958b) this measure has been used in experiments frequently. Although it correlates with skin conductance in most published studies (Mundy-Castle and McKiever, 1953; Sternbach, 1960; Lader, 1963) these correlations are of a low order and the measure justifies inclusion in its own right.

Techniques

There are many problems associated with the measurement of skin resistance and its derivations (Martin, 1967). The method used in these studies has been shown to be reliable, sensitive, and reproducible and is described elsewhere (Lader, 1963; Lader and Wing, 1966; Noble and Lader, 1971).

Recording

The subject sat in a comfortable chair and the electrode leads were plugged into position. Double-element electrodes (Lykken, 1959) were used so that a tetrapolar measuring system was created; a small current was passed through the outer system and the changes in resistance measured in the inner system and amplified by a Grass 5 polygraph. Using this system the artifacts due to back EMFs when a current is passed through the system do not affect the recorded resistance (Barnett, 1938). Calibration of the instrument was performed using the 100 kilohm resistor built into a Grass direct-coupled amplifier, and the voltage across the subject balanced back until the pen recorder of the driver amplifier traced a record close to the middle of the graph paper. The remaining voltage was then attenuated as required to give suitable range of resistance for the individual subject. Adjustments were made to the range as necessary during the period of recording as the pens used by Grass amplifiers are curvilinear; recording is at its most accurate near the middle of the range.

Recording took place during the reaction time task. The resistance was not only traced out by the pen of the Grass driver amplifier but also recorded on-line to the computer, where analogue to digital conversion was performed and the results stored on tape. The paper record was required to check the range of resistance during recording and also to calculate the number of fluctuations in skin resistance. The adjective 'spontaneous' has been omitted, because the fluctuations following the pressing of the key in the reaction-time task were included. It was often difficult to decide whether or not such fluctuations were spontaneous or related to the pressing of the key, and for this reason all fluctuations were summed. A change in conductance was recorded

as a fluctuation if it exceeded 0·004 log. micromhos of skin conductance i.e. 1 per cent of baseline.

The skin conductance, variance, and regression slope (habituation) were all derived from the raw resistance data using off-line analysis on the computer. The number of fluctuations per minute was also calculated.

2. Tremor

It has long been known that tremor may be a prominent symptom in anxiety. In the book of Ecclesiastes (12:i, iii) it is recorded that 'the keepers of the house shall tremble' at the thought of their creator, and the common expressions 'shivering with fear', 'quaking with horror', and 'chattering teeth' all illustrate the association between tremor and emotion. Like much that is common knowledge, however, the actual origins of the phenomenon are unknown although the increase of tremor that occurs in states of excitement is better understood. The earliest objective measurements of tremor were carried out in the 19th century by the tambour method, in which the movements of the trembling limb were transmitted by a rubber diaphragm to a pen, which traced out the movements on a smoked drum (Marey, 1868; Charcot, 1889). Considering the relative crudity of this method the results obtained were remarkably good. Charcot (1889) was able to divide pathological tremor into three groups based on frequency alone; slow (4–5 per second), equivalent to Parkinsonian tremor; intermediate (5½–6 per second), sometimes classed as 'hysterical'; and rapid or vibratory (8–9 per second), characteristic of thyrotoxicosis, alcoholism, and general paralysis of the insane. Later optical methods were used with some success. Most of these indirectly measured tremor displacement. The trembling part, usually the finger, interrupted a beam of light and this was recorded with a photo-electric device. All movement greater than a certain displacement was recorded and frequency could also be measured (Graham, 1945; Hammond, Merton, and Sutton, 1956; Redfearn, 1957). Other methods of measuring tremor include electromyographic techniques, pioneered by Schäfer, Canney, and Tunstall, (1886), who were the first to note a regular ten cycle/second rhythm in the electromyogram. Marshall and Walsh (1956) have used this technique in one of the most comprehensive studies of normal physiological tremor. Piezo-electric crystals (van Buskirk and Fink, 1962) and strain-gauges (Tuttle, Janney, Wilkerson, and Imig, 1951) have also been used with some success.

The technique used in the studies described in this book was the measurement of acceleration with a commercially available sub-miniature accelerometer (Ether BLA-2 model, Pye Industries Limited). This comprises two active inductive bridge arms, each wound within a magnetic shield. The air gap between the bridge arms is controlled by a seismically suspended magnetic armature. The accelerometer is supplied with only two bridge arms and it is necessary to make up the two remaining arms and incorporate a dry battery (1·5 volts) to complete the Wheatstone bridge. The accelerometer is light

(2·5 gm) and compact (1·7 mm × 0·7 mm × 0·5 mm) and is easily attached to the trembling part without altering the inertia of the system. The accelerometer only measures movement in the vertical plane so artifacts due to lateral movement are not recorded. The range of the accelerometer is much greater than that normally required for physiological purposes (±20 g) but it is sensitive to an accuracy of ±5 per cent and has a frequency spectrum of 1–100 Hz. The accelerometer has been used successfully in several studies of postural tremor Marsden, Meadows, Lange, and Watson, 1967; Marsden *et al.*, 1968; Marsden *et al.*, 1969a, 1969b) and gives reliable recordings.

Before recording the accelerometer was taped to the middle finger of the left hand immediately behind the finger-nail. The left forearm was supported to the level of the wrist-joint and the wrist fixed with a 'Velcro' band. The subject was asked to look straight ahead during the period of recording, when the left hand was held horizontal with the forearm pronated and the fingers slightly abducted. Preliminary tests showed that this gave consistent recordings.

The analogue signals representing acceleration of the trembling finger were amplified 10^3—10^4 times by a Grass P511C amplifier with the half-amplitude upper and lower frequencies set at 1000 Hz and 0·3 Hz respectively. The amplification factor was chosen after visual inspection of the acceleration on a Tektronix 502A oscilloscope. Recording lasted for about a minute on each occasion. During recording the analogue signals representing acceleration were filtered to allow only frequencies between 2 and 32 Hz to pass (Kemo Filters Limited), before on-line analysis with the computer. Attenuation beyond these frequencies was steep (36 db/octave). In the analysis eight 4·8 second epochs of tremor were displayed individually on the computer oscilloscope and any epochs containing artifacts rejected. After the full 40-second sample was obtained power spectral analysis was performed. This form of analysis is derived from communications engineering but has recently been applied with success to biological data. The principles of the technique have been given in detail (Blackman and Tukey, 1959), and its application in these studies described elsewhere (Tyrer and Bond, 1974; Tyrer and Lader, 1974c).

The power spectrum, which gave a measure of the amount of tremor at each frequency, was displayed on the computer oscilloscope in ½ Hz intervals between 1 and 32 Hz. The peaks of activity were separately recorded by setting cursors manually. A print-out of the activity in each Hz between 1 and 32 Hz was obtained before the values were stored on magnetic tape. Because diurnal variation has been demonstrated with physiological tremor (Tyrer and Bond, 1974) the time of recording for each experimental condition was kept the same in each of the studies described.

3. Tachycardia and Palpitations

Pulse rate is the easiest psychophysiological variable to measure. Most studies with anxious patients have shown significantly higher pulse rates in such patients than in control subjects (e.g. Wenger, 1948; Lader and Wing, 1966), but these changes are small and too variable to be of much clinical value (Altschule, 1953). It was essential to include pulse rate in the studies to be described for the obvious reason that beta-adrenergic blocking drugs primarily act on the cardiovascular system and have been shown to reduce pulse rate in anxious subjects to a significantly greater extent than in controls (Turner, Granville-Grossman, and Smart, 1965).

No other cardiovascular variables were measured. There were several reasons for this. Firstly, the symptoms of tachycardia and palpitations are experienced primarily as an increase in heart rate and to a lesser degree as an increase in force of cardiac contraction. There is no easy method of measuring cardiac output in a psychophysiological experiment and it is impossible to separate the contribution due to increased force from that due to increased rate. Other simple cardiovascular measures such as systolic and diastolic blood pressure, and skin blood flow, are not consciously perceived.

Technique

In the first experiment the radial pulse rate was measured by an independent assessor. In the later studies pulse rate was recorded on one of the channels of a Grass 5 polygraph. Conventional ECG electrodes were strapped to the upper forearm (so that they did not interfere with any of the other measures) after the electrode site had been prepared with Cambridge electrode jelly. The attached leads connected the electrodes to the input socket of a Grass 5P3 EMG preamplifier. The signals were attenuated so a clear record of pulse rate was traced out by the pen of a Grass driver amplifier. The tracing obtained approximated to the lead 1 ECG position in conventional terminology, in which there is normally a prominent QRS complex. At the speed of recording in the experiment (1·5 mm per second) this complex is normally reproduced as a straight line [Fig. 4].

Pulse rate was measured during the reaction-time task. The number of complexes in the 120 seconds following the first auditory click was counted and the average per minute calculated. The polygraph tracings were not analysed until after each subject had completed the experiment so that bias due to possible knowledge of drug effects was reduced to a minimum.

4. Respiration

It was decided to measure respiratory rate in the latter two studies in view of the known effects of beta-adrenergic blocking drugs on respiratory function (MacDonald, Ingram, and McNeill, 1967). Respiratory rate is a comparatively simple measure to record and although it has not received the same attention

as other psychophysiological variables its neglect does not necessarily reflect its value. Coppen and Mezey (1960) showed that in anxiety there was increased rate of respiration and that respiratory efficiency was impaired, and difficulty in breathing in one form or another is frequently related by anxious patients. Respiratory function in anxious patients has been claimed by Suzman (1968) to be significantly improved by the administration of propranolol although this was not supported by any objective tests.

Technique

A glass thermistor of resistance 2 kilohms (Type GB 32J1) (Fenwell Electronics Limited) was used. This is sensitive to small changes in temperature. The thermistor was set in a protective mount made of Araldite and added protection was given by setting the device in a rectangular block of polystyrene (1·5 cm × 0·5 cm × 0·5 cm). The leads from the thermistor were enclosed in an insulated cable and connected to a Grass low-level D.C.

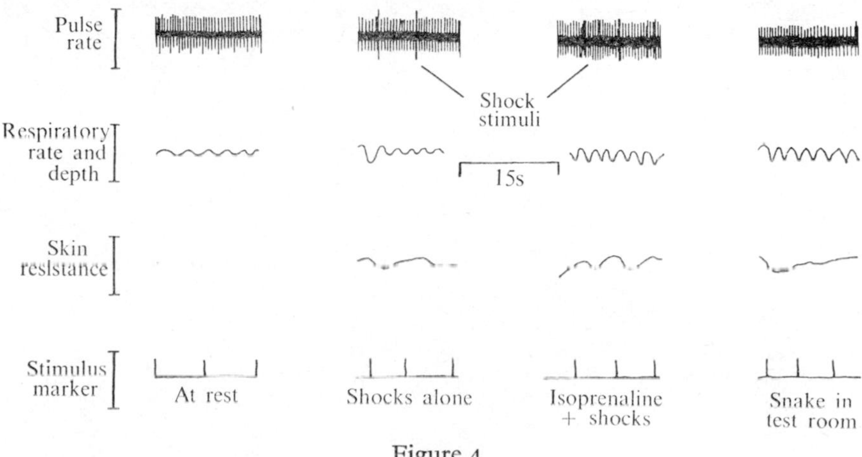

Figure 4

pre-amplifier (Model 5P1F). During recording the device was taped just below the nostril and the subject asked to breathe through his nose only. The attenuator and balancing system of the pre-amplifier were adjusted so that a smooth tracing of respiration was obtained from the pen of a Grass driver amplifier. When the subject breathes out the thermistor records a deflection in the tracing as the temperature rises, and a corresponding opposite deflection is shown when he inspires the relatively cooler external air. Sample tracings showing an increase during anxiety are shown [FIG. 4].

CENTRAL MEASURES

1. ELECTROENCEPHALOGRAM

The electroencephalogram (EEG) is the only true central measure available for psychophysiological study (Brown, 1967). Although it is an under-

standably primitive measure—few would hazard an interpretation of the workings of the internal combustion engine by listening with a stethoscope to its exterior—it has proved surprisingly useful in clinical neurology. In psychiatry, however, apart from diagnostic help in separating neurological conditions which present as psychiatric illness (e.g. the schizophrenia-like psychoses of epilepsy (Slater, Beard, and Glithero, 1963) its early promise has not been realized (Hill, 1963).

It does, however, show changes with certain drugs and during anxiety and so is relevant in the context of these experiments. In clinically anxious and anxiety-prone patients there is a reduction in the amount of alpha activity (Ulett, Gleser, Winokur, and Lawler, 1953) and an excess of faster activity (Heppenstall, Hill, and Slater, 1945; Brazier, Finesinger, and Cobb, 1945). These changes are not always present and are of doubtful clinical significance (Ellingson, 1954). Almost all psychoactive drugs have marked effects on the electroencephalogram. Those which are relevant in the context of anxiety include the barbiturates benzodiazepines and phenothiazines, and all of these produce changes in the electroencephalogram (Fink, 1969).

If beta-adrenergic blocking agents have central effects it is likely that similar changes would be shown in the electroencephalogram. If changes were not shown then subjective and behavioural effects would be difficult to relate to central action. This measure, more than any other, was therefore considered essential in the first study.

Technique

As drug-induced electroencephalographic changes show no evidence of localization it is not necessary to measure potential difference between many pairs of electrodes. In these experiments only two electrodes were used and their position determined by the need to maximize the evoked response to the auditory stimuli (see below). Bipolar silver—silver chloride pad electrodes were used. Before use they were soaked in saline solution. The electrode sites were the vertex (half-way between nasion and inion) and the left temporal region (two-fifths of distance along line drawn between the vertex and the left mastoid process). In the conventional 10–20 system (Jasper, 1958) these positions correspond to Cz and T3. The sites were prepared by first removing surface grease, using emery boards, cleaning the scalp with Hibitane and coating the area in contact with electrode jelly (Cambridge Instrument Company, Limited). The electrodes were held in position on the scalp by small bulldog clips attached to the hair. The electroencephalogram was amplified 10^5 times by a Grass P511C amplifier with the half-amplitude upper and lower frequencies set at 1000 Hz and 0·3 Hz respectively. The EEG was also displayed on a Tektronix 502A oscilloscope so that any artifacts (e.g. 50 Hz mains interference) could be corrected before the experiment began. The electroencephalogram was recorded during the reaction time task, and the sampling controlled by the computer. The experiments were run on-line.

A 5-second sample of electroencephalogram was analysed beginning 1 second after each auditory click. This was filtered through four parallal band-pass filters which divided the EEG into four frequency ranges; 2·4–4 Hz (roughly equivalent to the delta range), 4–7·5 Hz (theta range), 7·5–13·5 Hz (alpha range) and 13·5–26 Hz (approximating to the beta range). The outputs of the filters were rectified and at the end of the thirty-two samples the mean rectified voltage, and the mean total and percentage voltage in each frequency band calculated and stored on tape.

2. Auditory Evoked Response (AER)

The electroencephalographic evoked response to a variety of stimuli has received a great deal of attention in the past ten years. The lure of a physiological measure which offers the hope of quantifying such psychological states as attention, vigilance, and arousal has been too much to resist. It is not proposed to review the results of this work; it is difficult to assess because of wide contradictions in the conclusions of different workers, and the many different techniques used. Certainly, it has not lived up to the hopes of the early investigators and its value is still very limited. The measure did not receive close inquiry until Dawson (1951) showed that by summating electroencephalographic records the relatively small wave-form of the evoked response to a stimulus could be delineated. This method increases the relative size of the wave-form because the response is 'time-locked' to the stimulus. Thus when many samples of EEG are averaged the evoked responses are added together and eventually dominate the record, whereas the background EEG, which varies at random, shows little change. The application of computer techniques to averaging made measurement of the evoked response easier and widened the scope of research inquiry.

Unfortunately, the interpretations of the averaged wave-form are legion, and no standard method of measuring its individual components exists. The components measured in these studies derive from the work of Wilkinson (1967), who proposed that only four components of the evoked response had definite psychological significance, a peak at 60–70 msec (after an auditory click), P1, a trough at 100–120 msec, N1, another peak at 170–200 msec, P2, and another trough at 240–300 msec, N.2. Three amplitude of evoked response are derived from these, the P1N1 difference, the P2N1 difference and the P2N2 difference [Fig. 5].

There is evidence that the first of these amplitudes is dependent on selective attention (Satterfield, 1965) and the last of these (P2N2) is related to vigilance (Wilkinson, Morlock, and Williams, 1966). Known sedative drugs and anaesthetics tend to reduce all three of these amplitudes (Bergamasco, 1967; Domino, 1967; Lader and Norris, 1969; Jarvis and Lader, 1971) and so study of the amplitudes in particular was relevant to the investigation of central effects of beta-adrenergic blocking agents.

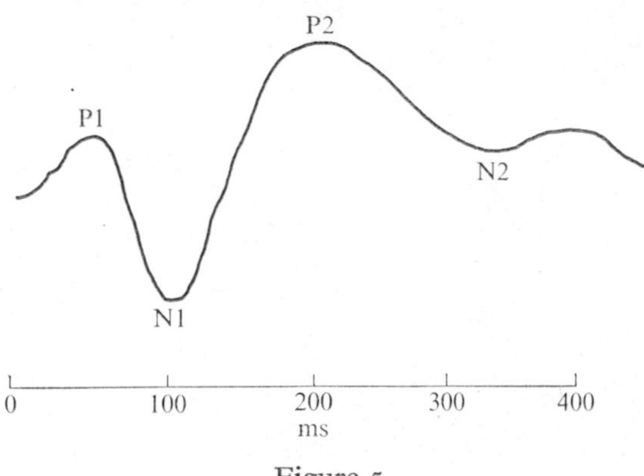

Figure 5

Technique

The auditory evoked response was measured during the reaction-time task. The pad electrodes were placed in the Cz–T3 positions to ensure that the vertex evoked response was recorded and to minimize artifacts arising from eye movements. Samples of electroencephalogram (500 msec) were recorded on-line to the computer, each sample beginning 20 msec before each of the thirty-two clicks. Each individual sample was displayed on the computer oscilloscope together with the reaction time to the click in milliseconds. If the reaction time exceeded 1 second (missed response) or if artifacts (usually due to muscle potentials) produced overflow in the record, the sample was discarded automatically. After all thirty-two samples had been collected they were averaged and the wave-form of the evoked response displayed on the computer oscilloscope. The total variance was also displayed. Cursors were adjusted manually so that the latencies of the four components, P1, N1, P2, and N2 were recorded. The voltage was also recorded at these latencies, so the amplitude of the P1 N1, P2 N1, and P2 N1 and P2 N2 waves was computed from these.

CHAPTER V

CENTRAL AND PERIPHERAL EFFECTS OF PROPRANOLOL AND SOTALOL AT REST

IT was emphasized in CHAPTER III that beta-adrenoceptor blocking drugs would be an inadequate means of investigating the role of bodily feelings in anxiety if they had central as well as peripheral effects. As a first priority it had to be established whether any of the subjective or physiological effects of propranolol and sotalol were central nervous system ones in nature. Previous evidence discussed in CHAPTER II showed that at low doses peripheral effects alone were detectable, at higher doses a variety of sedative and stimulant actions were present with different drugs and these appeared to be unrelated to beta-adrenoceptor blockade. Dosage was therefore an important factor in the experiment.

DESIGN OF STUDY

A cross-over design was chosen in which the effects of racemic propranolol (Inderal), racemic sotalol, and placebo were compared. A placebo control was clearly necessary to allow for the effects of non-specific factors in the experimental situation, as the 'placebo response' is very much a central phenomenon. Comparison between sotalol and propranolol allowed assessment of the possible relationship between membrane activity and central action.

A Latin square design using six subjects was used so that order effects were fully balanced. As there are marked inter-individual differences in physiological reactivity (Lacey, 1950) it is always preferable to measure drug effects within subjects wherever possible. Although it was appreciated that several of the behavioural measures in particular might show significant order effects due to practice, this alone would not justify changing the experimental design. Double-blind procedure was used throughout.

Six subjects (three male, three female) aged between 19 and 29 years, were each tested on three occasions one week apart. On each occasion the subject was tested three times; before, one hour, and three hours after taking an aqueous suspension of 120 mg racemic propranolol, 240 mg racemic sotalol, or placebo. The drugs were crushed and added to concentrated sweetened orange juice to disguise the bitter flavour that characterizes both propranolol and sotalol.

Subjects were asked to take no alcohol or any psychotropic drugs, including

hypnotics, during the 24 hours before testing. Because some individuals show excessive bradycardia after a small dose of a beta-adrenoceptor blocking drug (Fitzgerald, 1971), a test dose of 10 mg of racemic propranolol was given by mouth to all subjects several days before the experiment began and pulse rate measured at hourly intervals over the next 3 hours. No subjects experienced any untoward effects or showed marked bradycardia after the test dose, so it was felt safe to give the full experimental dose. None of the subjects suffered from asthma or cardiac disease.

The dosage chosen was moderately large. This was deliberate. Sotalol was ascribed a potency of half that of propranolol on the basis of clinical experience in man (Prichard, personal communication). This is not an ideal method of determining potency but was considered preferable to the alternative based on animal pharmacology. These suggest that sotalol is only $\frac{1}{8}$ to $\frac{1}{16}$ as potent as propranolol in its cardiac effects (Fitzgerald, 1969; Gomoll, 1970). *In vivo*, however, sotalol appears to be considerably more potent, possibly because of superior absorption and greater metabolic stability. For example, in one study sotalol was shown to be more potent than propranolol following oral administration in dogs (Lish, Shelanski, LaBudde, and Williams, 1967). Because of these conflicting results it was decided to rely on clinical experience in determining approximately equipotent doses.

Experimental Procedure

All subjects were shown the experimental equipment and the procedure was described before they were tested for the first time. The procedure was identical on each test occasion. The subject sat in a comfortable chair in a sound-protected room and was allowed to relax before testing began. Each test followed the procedure described in Chapter IV and was given in the order shown below.

(*a*) Power spectral analysis of resting electroencephalogram (40 secs)
(*b*) Power spectral analysis of finger tremor (40 secs)
(*c*) Recording of electroencephalogram
(*d*) Reaction time
(*e*) Skin conductance
(*f*) Auditory evoked response
} carried out simultaneously during the reaction-time task
(*g*) Key tapping
(*h*) Radial pulse rate. An independent assessor recorded the pulse rate for 60 seconds.

After these tests were completed, 10 ml of venous blood was taken from the subject (except on the pre-drug occasion), the placebo sample was discarded and the drug samples were stored as whole blood at 4° C. The remaining tests were carried out in a separate room.

(*i*) Subjective mood scale
(*j*) Bodily symptom scale

been suggested that an equipotent dose of sotalol in man is 1 to 1½ times that of propranolol (Svedmyr, Jacobsson, and Malmberg, 1969), in which case the 2:1 ratio in this experiment would have been too large. It is possible that both drugs were given in doses close to the threshold at which central effects occur, propranolol in a sub-threshold dose and sotalol in a supra-threshold one, and so only sotalol showed definite evidence of sedation.

It is fair to conclude that racemic propranolol has no important central effects after 120 mg in acute dosage in normal subjects. The important question of whether the beta-adrenoceptor blocking drugs are appropriate agents to study bodily feelings in anxiety is therefore answered, but careful attention to dosage is essential. In a dose of 120 mg propranolol produces no significant side effects and most subjects are unaware that they had taken an active drug at all. Physiological tests confirm the absence of central effects. Therefore, any changes shown in normal subjects or patients in dosage at or below this level are possibly due to peripheral pharmacological action.

On the other hand racemic sotalol has central effects suggestive of a depressant action on the central nervous system after 240 mg in acute dosage. It would thus be unwise to give a dose as large as this in other studies as central effects could not be differentiated from peripheral ones. Although sotalol is alleged to be a pure beta-adrenoceptor blocking agent it does have properties independent of beta-blocking activity at high dosage and so 'purity' is only relative.

These were the chief points to be considered in planning further investigations. The results of the experiment also illustrated that the combined approach of physiological and psychological recordings was useful and sensitive to change but that these could not be correlated with the pharmacokinetics of propranolol with the measures available. Plasma levels of racemic propranolol showed no correlation with pulse rate, presumably because other active metabolites were contributing to beta-blockade.

CHAPTER VI

A CLINICAL STUDY OF SOTALOL AND PLACEBO IN CHRONIC ANXIETY

THE work described in the previous chapter suggested that central action did not contribute to any anti-anxiety effects of beta-adrenoceptor blocking drugs. However, it is unwise to draw general conclusions from results obtained with a single fixed dose of any drug in normal volunteers. A second study was therefore carried out in patients with pathological anxiety in which sotalol was taken in flexible dosage for two weeks. Flexible dosage was considered preferable because the dose chosen by patients would give an indication of which pharmacological actions of sotalol were clinically important. If central sedative effects were beneficial one would expect patients to prefer a much greater mean dosage than if effects due to beta-adrenoceptor blockade were the most important. Because of this, a wide dosage range of sotalol was chosen. The design was determined by the need to compare the results with those of previous studies. As both of the important trials of beta-adrenergic blocking agents in the treatment of anxiety (Granville-Grossman and Turner, 1966; Bonn *et al.*, 1972) employed a sequential design (Armitage, 1960), a similar design was chosen in the study with sotalol. Sequential designs may be used to compare the effects of treatment between groups of patients or within groups of patients using a cross-over design. A cross-over design is only justified if it can be confidentially predicted that there will be no 'carry-over' effects from treatment to treatment. Such a prediction could be made with sotalol provided that patients with chronic anxiety were being treated. Patients with acute anxiety show a tendency to improve spontaneously and apparent treatment effects may be long-lasting (Rickels, Lipman, and Raab, 1966). This probably accounts for the significant differences between order of treatment in the first trial of propranolol in anxiety (Granville-Grossman and Turner, 1966).

The patients included in the study were all out-patients attending the Maudsley Hospital. All were required to have had morbid anxiety as a major symptom for at least six months before assessment. Patients with other psychiatric disorders (e.g. depression, schizophrenia) were excluded and the final group of fourteen patients who completed the trial comprised nine patients with chronic anxiety states, three with agoraphobia (which often coexists with an anxiety state) and two with primary personality disorders. All had previously received treatment with anxiety-reducing drugs without lasting benefit. Six were male, eight were female; the mean age was 39·1 years

(s.d 12·1) and the mean duration of symptoms was 7·6 years. In most patients treatment with sotalol was considered as an alternative to conventional treatment with anxiolytic drugs as the latter had failed to alleviate symptoms, or had produced unpleasant side-effects. In this respect the population studied was not only chronically anxious but might also be regarded as more refractory than most patients with anxiety.

METHOD

A restricted sequential design ($\theta = 0{\cdot}90$, $2\times = 0{\cdot}05$, $\beta = 0{\cdot}05$) (see Armitage, 1960) was used to determine the number of patients entering the trial. Each patient took sotalol and matching tablets of placebo, each for two weeks in flexible dosage. After each patient had completed the two treatments, both therapist and subject made a preference for the more effective treatment. If there was no difference between the treatments this could also be recorded [FIG. 7]. The trial was terminated when a boundary was crossed.

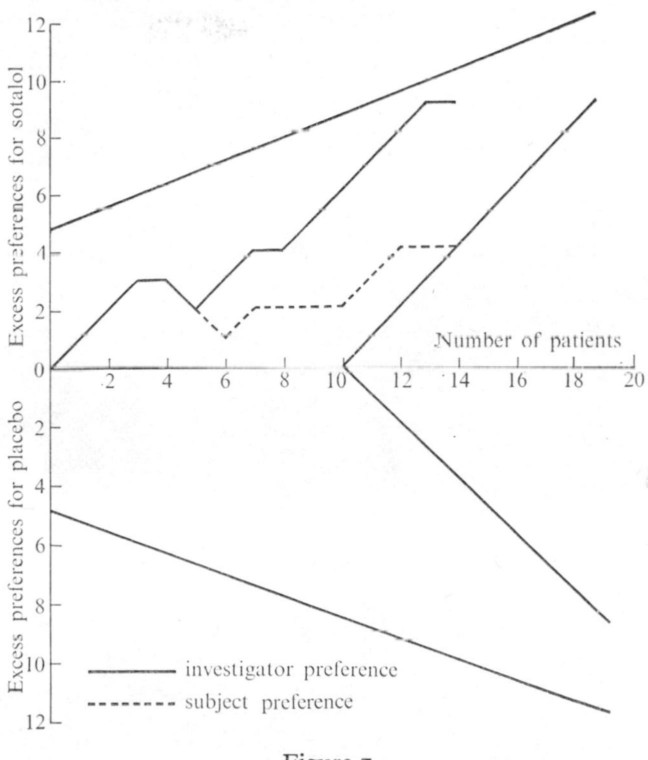

Figure 7

No other drugs were allowed during the trial apart from hypnotics when indicated. Only three patients needed hypnotics, two taking nitrazepam (Mogadon) and one triclofos (Tricloryl) throughout the period of study.

The treatments were administered in random order and their allocation determined by the staff of the pharmacy at the Maudsley Hospital. At the

start of the study the permitted dosage range was 80–800 mg daily in divided dosage (q.d.s.); the maximum dose was lowered to 400 mg daily after the fifth patient to enter the trial dropped out of treatment. The tablets were made up in bottles each containing 250 20 mg tablets. Additional bottles containing 100 mg tablets of sotalol or placebo were also available for patients who preferred a higher dose range. The bottles were returned after treatment and the mean daily dosage calculated by counting the unused tablets. Most patients preferred the lower dosage range and the mean daily dose was 124 mg of sotalol. Venous blood samples were taken for toxicological tests after each treatment.

The ratings used were the Hamilton Rating Scale for Anxiety and the self-rating scales of subjective mood and bodily symptoms already described [CHAPTER IV]. These were completed before treatment and after each drug. Patients were all drug-free at the time of initial assessment. The only objective measure included was finger tremor. This was included because of its possible clinical relevance. Although there have been no studies of the effect of beta-blockade on tremor in anxiety in the long term, the work of Marsden and his colleagues (Marsden *et al.*, 1968) suggests that propranolol in acute dosage reduces tremor in anxiety; this observation had not been confirmed in a psychiatric population with neurotic anxiety, and such an investigation was clearly indicated. The technique for measuring tremor was as described in CHAPTER IV.

RESULTS

The trial was completed after 14 patients had completed treatment and the results of the sequential analysis are shown in FIGURE 7. After the fourteenth patient had made a treatment preference the line indicating patient preference reached an inner boundary. It was decided not to continue with the trial even though the therapist's preference was close to an upper boundary. Although it could be argued that the therapist preference was more accurate (psychiatrists are usually considered to be better judges of symptoms than patients) this was open to doubt in this particular instance. It is easy to make the unwarranted assumption that patients who notice a reduction in autonomic symptoms are therefore improved. On several occasions patients regarded this reduction in symptoms as irrelevant to their anxiety and in no way felt the altered symptomatology was therapeutic. In such cases the observed emotional behaviour and symptomatology may have been misleading because of the effects of beta-blockade. In a drug-free patient the external observer is a more accurate assessor of overt emotion than the subject experiencing it (Hebb, 1946a). Beta-adrenoceptor blockade masks some of the important features which the observer relies on in making his assessment and so in this instance the subjective account was considered more important.

These comments must be borne in mind when considering the other results of the trial. The rating scores and tremor data were subjected to a split-plot

analysis of variance, both the drugs and order effects being estimated against within-patients residual variance. The Hamilton ratings [Fig. 8] showed marked drug-placebo differences for a number of symptoms but because of the strictures made above about the accuracy of observer assessment, not too much reliance can be placed on these. The interview in which the Hamilton ratings were assessed was a semi-structured one in which the patient first described his symptoms and progress before the individual questions on the scale were asked. In some instances an apparent reduction in bodily symptoms

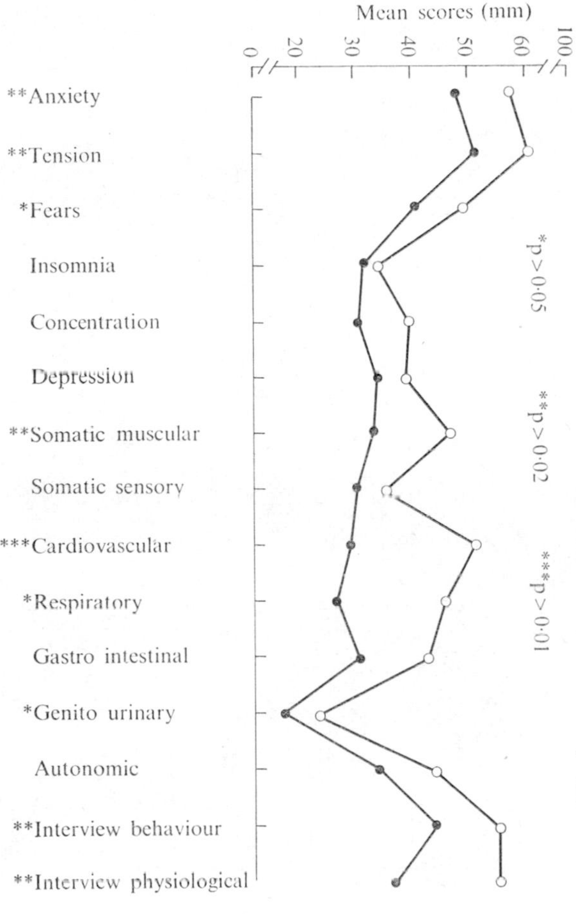

Figure 8

or external appearance of reduced anxiety could have influenced the rating for a symptom such as anxiety or tension. The ratings for the autonomic symptoms may also have been affected by this procedure.

The patients' own ratings of bodily symptoms did not show significant treatment differences [Table 5]. This result was surprising, as my (therapist) assessments had apparently detected changes in several of these symptoms. One reason may be that subjective assessment of such symptoms may be

unreliable (Mandler, Mandler, and Uviller, 1958; Mandler and Kremen, 1958) and another may be that the distribution of these ratings is markedly skewed, and so a logarithmic or arc sin transformation should have been carried out before analysis. The skew distribution was confirmed in a later experiment [CHAPTER VII], and logarithmic transformation of these ratings was performed in the latter studies.

Another reason for the failure to show significant differences may be that bodily feelings were rated at a single point in time—when completing the scale—rather than an assessment over the two-week period of drug treatment. If subjective awareness of bodily feelings fluctuated greatly during the course of the day then the rating at a single point in time would not be representative. There is some evidence that wide fluctuation in bodily feelings does occur in

TABLE 5 EFFECTS OF SOTALOL ON SELF-RATINGS OF BODILY SYMPTOMS

	MEAN RATING (0–100 MM)		
BODILY SYMPTOM	Sotalol	Placebo	F-RATIO
Sweating	38·3	39·4	0·02
Trembling	37·1	40·8	0·13
Palpitations	32·6	46·2	2·34
Nausea	30·4	30·9	0·00
Diarrhoea	14·6	20·7	1·08
Genito-urinary	28·3	21·9	1·07
Difficulty in breathing	33·9	27·5	0·53
Muscular tension	52·1	43·3	1·34

None of the ratings showed significant changes between placebo and sotalol. For 1 and 12 degrees of freedom an F-ratio has to exceed 4·84 to be significant at the 0·05 level of probability.

anxiety from the ratings of another patient with chronic anxiety who completed ratings of mood and bodily symptoms four times daily for four weeks [FIG. 9]. Changes in subjective anxiety are much more gradual and show less fluctuation than mean bodily symptom ratings.

The patients' ratings of mood showed the most interesting treatment differences [FIG. 10]. These differences are not great and were not sufficient to affect the patients' overall preferences in the sequential analysis. However, patients were significantly calmer, happier, more contented and quick-witted when taking sotalol than when taking placebo and this could hardly be a chance finding. FIGURE 8 shows that these differences were only relative; the mean ratings on sotalol for each of these facets of mood show that relief of anxiety and other symptoms were only partial.

There was also a significant reduction in tremor (F = 5·1, d.f. 1, 12;

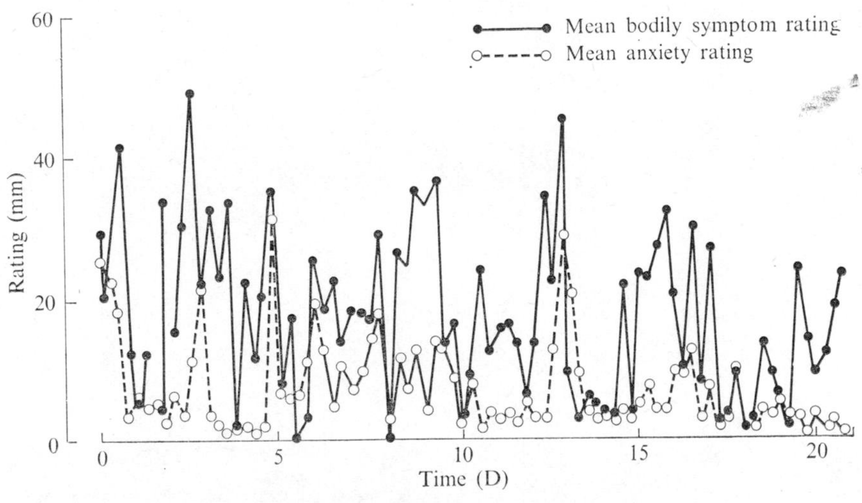

Figure 9

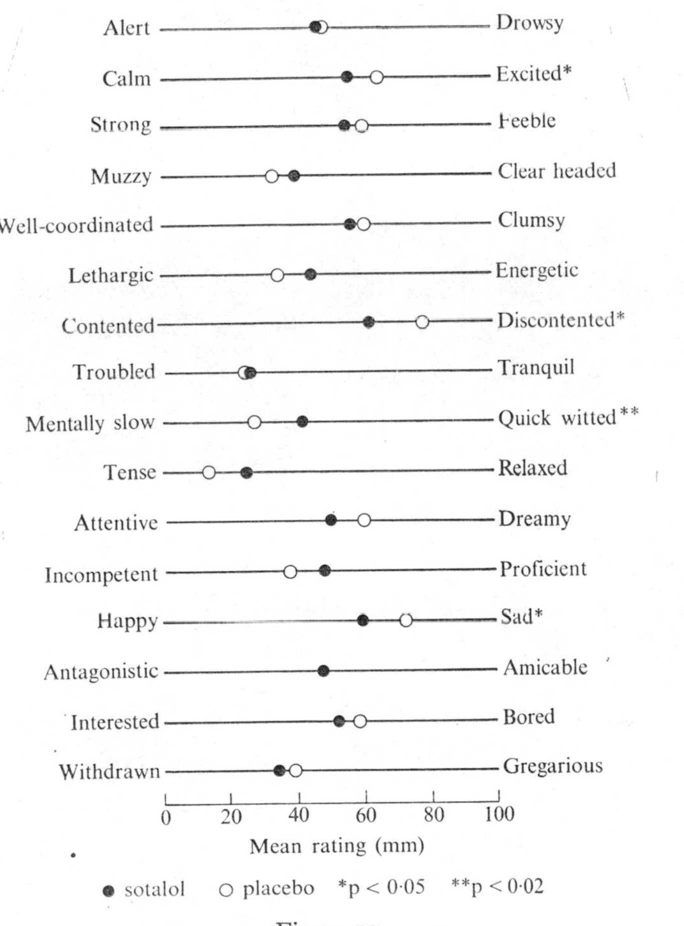

Figure 10

$p < 0{\cdot}05$) [Fig. 11]. This confirmed the findings of Marsden *et al.* (1968) that beta-blockade reduced the excessive tremor in anxiety. It is difficult to know to what extent this was related to the improvement in mood, particularly as subjective ratings of tremor showed no significant differences. Nevertheless two patients spontaneously reported that they felt better because their tremor was less marked.

There were no unwanted effects in eleven of the patients, two complained of symptoms undistinguishable from those of anxiety (particularly headaches, blurring of vision and nausea) while taking placebo, and one complained of

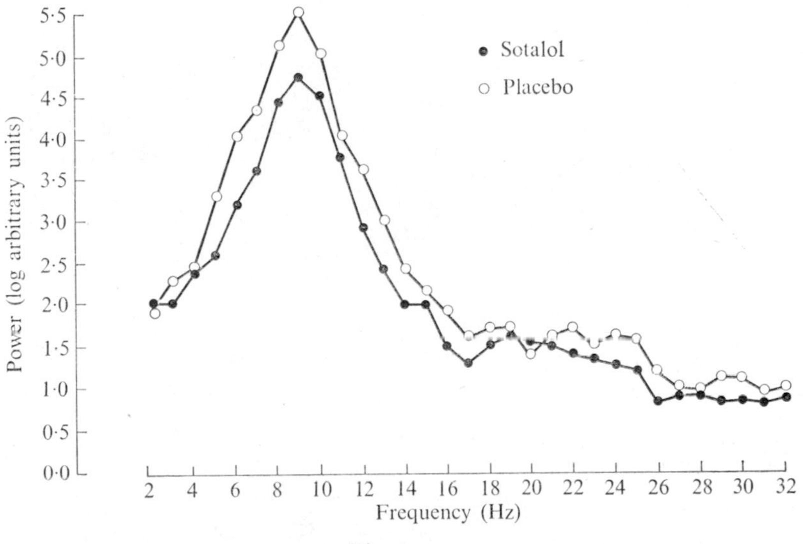

Figure 11

respiratory difficulty while taking sotalol. The fifth patient to enter the trial dropped out after experiencing hypnagogic and hypnopompic hallucinations. These symptoms occurred after she had been taking 600 mg of sotalol daily for three days. They included visual hallucinations (the patient woke up and saw figures walking round her bedroom) and auditory hallucinations (voices shouting aggressively at her and repeating her name). No perceptual symptoms had ever been experienced before this occasion. The patient related these phenomena to her anxiety and took more sotalol the next day, but the following night she experienced these symptoms again. She stopped taking sotalol after this and the symptoms did not recur. It was impossible to avoid the conclusion that sotalol was responsible for these hallucinatory phenomena, and so it appears that sotalol is similar in this regard to propranolol (Stephen, 1966; Hinshelwood, 1969; Zacharias *et al.*, 1972). Because of this episode the maximum permitted dose of sotalol was lowered to 400 mg daily. Another patient dropped out after complaining of 'pricking feelings like electric shocks' in her limbs while taking sotalol 160 mg daily.

Only four of the fourteen patients felt sufficiently improved on sotalol to

continue taking it after the trial was completed. The improvement of two of these was not maintained and alternative treatment was necessary, so that six weeks after completion of the trial only two patients were still taking sotalol. Although this is an unimpressive result it must be taken into account that the patients were a therapeutically refractory group in which any improvement was considered to be an achievement. Both patients who continued to take sotalol suffered from generalised anxiety and phobic symptoms, and found the main benefit of the drug was the quelling of panicky feelings in their phobic situations.

Conclusions

It is difficult to interpret the results of the trial in isolation. Of all the rating methods, the sequential analysis was the most relevant from a clinical viewpoint and this showed sotalol to be relatively ineffective. The ratings of mood and Hamilton ratings did show significant drug-placebo differences, however, and tremor was also reduced. Sotalol in patients with chronic anxiety does therefore have effects of potential benefit but these were not perceived as anxiety-relieving in many of the patients.

One possible cause of the differences in benefit might have been different dosage in those patients who improved, as compared with those who did not. The mean dosage taken in each of the patients was therefore examined separately to see if it was related to improvement. Tremor values were also included as greater reduction in tremor might occur if tremor reduction was dose-related. There was no evidence that dose or tremor reduction was primarily responsible for improvement as there was little difference in these variables in the improved and unimproved groups [Table 6].

TABLE 6 MEAN DOSAGE OF SOTALOL AND AMOUNT OF TREMOR IN SUBJECTIVE RESPONDERS AND NON-RESPONDERS

GROUP (BASED ON SUBJECTIVE PREFERENCE IN TRIAL)	NUMBER	MEAN DAILY DOSAGE OF SOTALOL (MG)	MEAN TREMOR ($\log_e$ units)	
			Placebo	Sotalol
Sotalol preference	6	129	7·1	6·7
Placebo preference	2	109	7·2	6·9
No preference	6	124	7·4	6·6

No evidence of an increased reduction in tremor or differing dosage of sotalol is shown in the three groups.

The explanation for the improvement in mood with sotalol is also not apparent. As the mean dosage of sotalol was so low, however, it is extremely unlikely that the mechanism of the mood change is a central nervous one. A reasonable conclusion is that beta-adrenoceptor blockade may directly lead to a lessening of subjective anxiety but the evidence is disturbingly circumstantial and tells us nothing about the processes involved. The results

of this study are similar to those of previous work (Granville-Grossman and Turner, 1966; Bonn *et al.*, 1972) but the additional information provided by assessment with many scales suggests that it is not enough to reduce autonomic symptomatology in an anxious patient to produce improvement. Because of this the subject's preference has been given more weight than my own in assessing the results. In other trials the subjects' own preference was not included in the published reports, although this was recorded in the results of one of these trials and found to be much less impressive than the results of investigator preference (Bonn, personal communication). It is important not to assume that a reduction in the external manifestations of anxiety is automatically associated with relief of anxiety. One expects from the known pharmacological effects of beta-blockade [CHAPTER II] that some of the characteristic clinical features of anxiety may be affected. This may contaminate the judgement of an observer so that he concludes that improvement has occurred. It is easy to see that unaltered subjective anxiety combined with less observed anxiety may be recorded as an improvement—the player wears a mask which apparently hides his true feelings. Patients' own ratings are free from any such contamination and in the special case of assessment of beta-adrenoceptor blockade in anxiety they are preferable to ratings based on psychiatric assessment.

The mode of action of sotalol in its effects on mood does not appear to be a simple reduction of learned associations between bodily symptoms and anxiety which would be predicted from the views of Richter (1940) and Breggin (1964). Patients' own ratings of bodily symptoms did not show much improvement on sotalol and although this could be partly due to the absence of appropriate statistical conversion and wide variations in symptomatology throughout the day, these ratings were completed at the same time as those of mood. If there is a direct relationship between reduction of bodily symptoms and relief of anxiety it remains hidden from the results of this study.

The next phase of investigation was the measurement of anxiety and bodily feelings more frequently and under more controlled conditions so that their interdependence could come under closer scrutiny.

CHAPTER VII

THE IMPORTANCE OF BODILY FEELINGS IN INDUCED ANXIETY

To test the effects of drugs on bodily feelings and mood in normal anxiety it is necessary to have an experimental design in which anxiety can be easily and reliably reproduced. A clinical trial over a long period is seldom appropriate because it is almost impossible to create an anxiety-inducing situation which will persist for more than several hours. Attempts have been made to study the effects of drugs on anxiety in real-life situations (e.g., Walk, 1956; Fenz and Epstein, 1967) but with most such situations there are difficulties in repeating measurements on other occasions and in standardizing the stress variable. Because of this, most experiments with normal subjects employ single dose administration or intravenous infusion of the drug under test. The stress situations are standardised and subjects are exposed to them for a short period. This kind of design lends itself to experimental manipulation and is particularly useful when cross-over designs are chosen.

There were other factors which influenced the choice of stressful procedure and experimental design in this study. The type of stress chosen had to be one which would not significantly interfere with the recording of physiological measures, which excluded all those in which the subject is required to be mobile. The other important factor was the known tendency of individuals to respond to stress physiologically in a specific way (Lacey, 1950; Lacey and van Lehn, 1952; Lacey, Bateman, and van Lehn, 1953; Lacey and Lacey, 1958a). Comparison of physiological measurements between different groups of subjects under stress conditions is therefore not appropriate unless individual idiosyncrasies are taken into account.

DESIGN OF STUDY

A. Drugs

Three active drugs and placebo were compared. Racemic propranolol had been shown to have no central effects in a single dose of 120 mg in the first study [Chapter V] and so this drug was tested again. Again a dose of 120 mg was chosen as it was felt necessary to get the maximum degree of beta-blockade without producing central effects. Sotalol had been shown in the first experiment to be a less 'pure' beta-blocking agent than was at first thought and so the dextro-isomer of propranolol was chosen for comparison. There are several advantages in this. The dextro-isomer (dexpropranolol or

d-propranolol) has only $\frac{1}{60}$th to $\frac{1}{100}$th of the beta-adrenoceptor blocking activity of the l-isomer (Howe and Shanks, 1966; Barrett and Cullum, 1968) but in other pharmacological actions it is very similar. Therefore if a particular pharmacological property is shown by the racemic mixture but not by *d*-propranolol then the action demonstrated is probably due to beta-blockade.

The third drug compared was the benzodiazepine, diazepam (Valium). The benzodiazepines are now the most commonly prescribed anti-anxiety agents and diazepam is a typical member of the group. In animal experiments it has been shown that the drug has a central rather than a peripheral action (Schallek and Zabransky, 1966; Chai and Wang, 1966) and this is consistent with its clinical effects in man (Jenner and Kerry, 1967). The drug has been used in the treatment of disorders which can be loosely grouped as psychosomatic, particularly non-specific gastro-intestinal complaints (Voegtlin, 1964) and cardiovascular complaints such as neurocirculatory asthenia (Cromwell, 1963). Although the therapeutic action in these conditions is probably a central one, it is still possible that a peripheral action is partly responsible. Whatever the mechanism of action, and on balance it is very difficult to argue that it is primarily a peripheral one, it is valuable to compare its effects with propranolol under controlled conditions.

A comparison with placebo was essential for many reasons. Quite apart from the need to compare the effects of the drugs with an agent which has no pharmacological action, the design chosen (see below) allowed for many non-specific sources of variation in drug effects and it was essential to control for these as well. The drugs were made up in identical white capsules containing diazepam (2 mg), *d*-1-propranolol (40 mg), *d*-propranolol (40 mg), and placebo.

B. Stressful Situations

Three different situations were chosen.

(i) *Electric shocks alone*

Electric shocks have been used to induce anxiety and fear in psychological experiments for many years. The technique has been used particularly in experimental psychology because of its simplicity and reliability in creating anxiety and increased arousal (Spence, Farber, and Taylor, 1954; Hilgard, 1956; Caldwell and Cromwell, 1959). It is more limited in human studies because of wide inter-individual variations in response to shocks, and because of habituation following repeated administration. As much anxiety appears to be created by the threat of shock as by the shock itself (Spence, 1964).

In this experiment the shocks were administered from a purpose-built battery operated unit. This consisted of a PP9 battery (9 volts) connected to a 1:70 transformer and a series of resistances, one of which was adjustable so that the current could be altered. A dial marked from 0 to 10 showed the range of the adjustable resistance, which allowed any current between 4 and

100 milliamperes to pass between the two electrodes. The shocks were triggered simultaneously with the clicks by the computer via a Devices digitimer.

The shocks were given during the reaction time task [CHAPTER IV]. On the first occasion that the subject received shocks there was a dummy run of this part of the experiment. The subject made no response to the auditory clicks and the voltage of the shocks, administered at the same time as the clicks, was adjusted until the subject indicated that the feeling of the shock was unpleasant but not unbearable. The voltage level was noted and on all later occasions the subject received the same voltage. This did not necessarily mean that the current between the electrodes remained the same; if the skin resistance altered it is apparent from Ohm's law that the current would alter accordingly. To reduce these changes to a minimum the shock electrodes were placed close to the ECG electrode on the left upper arm and both held in position with the same rubber strap. It has to be noted, however, that Allen, Armstrong-Roddie (1973) have shown that the upper arm is involved in emotional sweating. However, during the experiment none of the subjects wanted to have the voltage level altered because the shocks were too unpleasant so a difficult ethical problem did not arise.

(ii) *Electric shocks and isoprenaline*

It is very difficult to assess how much of the feelings experienced in anxiety are due to circulating catecholamines and how much derives from other sources. There is no doubt that the secretion of catecholamines, particularly adrenaline, is increased in anxiety and that exogenous administration of catecholamines increases pre-existing anxiety (see discussion in CHAPTER II). It was decided to include the administration of isoprenaline as one of the stressful procedures because (*a*) it is the prototype beta-agonist, (*b*) from the work of Schachter and Singer (1962) it would be predicted that in an anxiety-inducing situation isoprenaline would increase anxiety and its bodily accompaniments, and (*c*) comparison with the results of other stressful procedures might give some indication of the extent that catecholamines are involved in normal anxiety. In this part of the experiment the dice were effectively loaded in favour of racemic propranolol. If bodily symptoms caused by catecholamines were very important in the genesis of anxiety then it would be expected that propranolol would show marked benefit.

Isoprenaline may be administered as tablets (short or long-acting), by aerosol inhaler or by intravenous drip. The last method was excluded for several reasons, the chief of which was the subjective unpleasantness of the procedure (Fowle, personal communication), but it also posed technical difficulties. The other methods of administration are less reliable because absorption is erratic and varies from individual to individual. Absorption by aerosol inhaler was preferred because the drug is absorbed quickly and the effect of a single dose is short-lasting. It was important for the effects of isoprenaline not to be shown in the later parts of the experiment so under the

circumstances administration by aerosol was essential. A commercially manufactured preparation was used (Medihaler Iso Forte—Riker Laboratories Limited), which contains 20 mg isoprenaline per ml.

The isoprenaline was given immediately before the experimental procedure. The subject was taught how to use the inhaler and one or two metered doses given (0·5–1·5 mg), depending on the immediate subjective response. The number of doses was noted and on the second occasion the subject was tested the same dose was given. The method of analysis of the results reduced inter-individual variation to a minimum (see below). The rest of the experiment was conducted in the same way as the procedure with electric shocks alone. Shocks at the same voltage were administered during the reaction-time task; the difference between the effects of 'isoprenaline plus shocks' and 'shocks alone' showed the contribution isoprenaline was making to the stressful procedure. Because of the known effects of suggestion and mental set in stress situations (Schachter and Singer, 1962) the subjects were merely told that the isoprenaline 'might affect some of their feelings'. The results showed that the aerosol was an appropriate method of giving the isoprenaline; anxiety was rather more pronounced than for the electric shocks alone, but not greatly so [FIG. 6].

(iii) *Phobic situation*

Anxiety in real life differs from that induced in an experimental situation. Because of this it was decided to include a form of stress which more closely resembled real anxiety. Phobias are good examples; they have the advantage of easy reproducibility in an experimental situation and, provided that exposure to them is not too prolonged (Watson, Gaind, and Marks, 1971), they show little habituation with successive exposures to the phobic stimulus. The kind of phobias that could be tested were limited. If they were too frightening the subjects would not be able to perform the other parts of the experiment and artifacts would occur in the physiological recordings. The phobic stimulus had to be one which could be introduced into the testing booth, so such phobias as those of heights, large dogs, thunder and lightning, and speaking in public had to be excluded. Of the thirty-two subjects tested, 16 (50 per cent) had a fear of snakes, 8 (25 per cent) had fears in social situations, 4 (12½ per cent) had rat phobia, 2 (6 per cent) had a fear of spiders, 1 (3 per cent) a fear of bursting balloons, and 1 (3 per cent) an examination phobia. Of these, 5 subjects had symptoms of such severity as to warrant a formal diagnosis of monosymptomatic phobia.

Fortunately an animal house was in the same building as the experimental laboratory and both rats and snakes were easily available. The snake used in the experiments was a tame boa constrictor, which was either kept in a cage or allowed to roam loose in the testing booth depending on the tolerance of the subject. White rats, chiefly large Wistar rats, were obtained for subjects with rat phobias. The testing booth was fitted with a one way screen so that the

subject could be observed during the experiment. If the animals showed any tendency to interfere with the other parts of the experiment (e.g. by interfering with the reaction time task) the computer was temporarily halted and the animal moved to a less threatening position. Those subjects with social fears had the appropriate situation reproduced as accurately as possible in the experiment. In most instances the subject was stared at by one or more people seated in front of or beside him. One restriction was that the people acting as phobic stimuli were not allowed to talk during the experiment as this could have interfered with the responses in a way independent of the anxiety induced. The spiders obtained were large specimens of the common house spider (*Tegenaria domestica*), a web-weaving spider noted for its long legs and speed of movement when aroused. One subject could not tolerate a live spider and dead carcasses were used. Balloons were inflated and burst just outside the door of the test room for the subject who was afraid of sudden noises and the final subject with an examination phobia was played a tape recording during the experiment in which the scene of a forthcoming examination was recreated and the likelihood of failure emphasized throughout.

The three stress situations were produced in the same order for each subject. They were preceded and followed by testing at rest with the same experimental procedure. Thus there were five test situations in all.

C. Experimental Design

Mention has already been made of the difficulty in comparing physiological responses between individuals because of autonomic response stereotypy. Because of this it was decided to test each subject on two separate days. On the first occasion the subject took no drug and was tested five times in the situations described above. On the second occasion the prodecure was repeated using identical stress stimuli except that on this occasion the subject took a drug after the first test situation so the remaining four times of testing could be influenced by drug effects. To minimize the variance due to autonomic specificity the statistical analysis was carried out on the change scores between the first and second occasions, and to reduce the influence of habituation between the two periods of testing these scores were themselves subjected to change scores. The scores of the four drug-influenced situations were subtracted from the score on the first time of testing. The description of this analysis may appear unnccessarily complex but it is easily expressed diagrammatically:

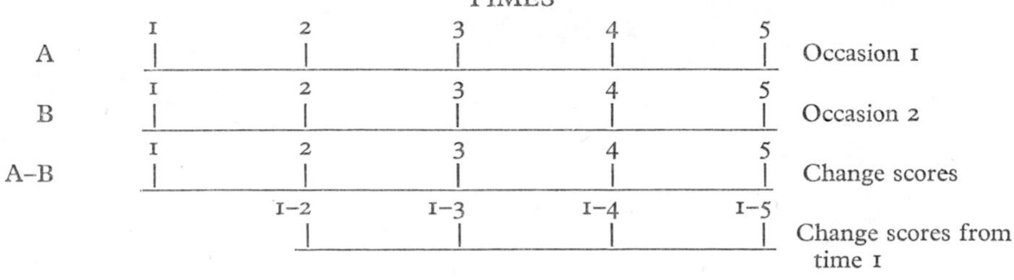

Thus the original set of ten recordings from each subject was reduced to four in the analysis of the results. It was realized that this could lead to some loss of sensitivity, particularly for those measures such as subjective ratings which can be compared more appropriately than physiological responses, but it was hoped that this would be offset by lessened variance. Because habituation to the stress procedures was expected, each subject was tested twice only, once with and once without a drug. A cross-over design was not chosen for this experiment because it was anticipated that the order effects due to habituation would be much greater than those due to drug effects. Thirty-two paid volunteer subjects were tested; these comprised sixteen males and sixteen females aged between 18 and 38 years (chiefly medical students and post-graduate research workers). These were equally divided into four groups, each containing four male and four female subjects, and allotted to the four different treatments, placebo, *d*-propranolol, *d*-1-propranolol and diazepam. The allocation of subjects was carried out by an independent observer; the initial allocation for treatment was a random one, but later subjects sometimes had to be included in a particular group so that the sexes were equally distributed in the final sample.

An analysis of variance was carried out on the change scores. This was a split-plot analysis, the F-ratio for the drug groups being estimated against between subject error variance and those for the drug $\times$ times interaction being estimated against within times, within subject error variance.

D. Physiological and Psychological Measures

The subjective mood and bodily symptom scales had been shown to be useful in the previous studies and these were used again. An external rating of mood was not included. The performance tasks were unaffected by propranolol in the first experiment but three of these, reaction time, tapping, and the symbol copying test (SCT) were included to see whether diazepam in the dose given had any effects on performance. The peripheral physiological measures of skin conductance, finger tremor, pulse rate, and respiratory rate were all recorded as described in Chapter IV. Wave-band analysis of the electroencephalogram and the averaged evoked response to the auditory clicks were also recorded. These will not be discussed further here as they were included to assess the effects of diazepam rather than either of the isomers of propranolol. The results in fact confirmed those of the first experiment, neither *d*-propranolol nor *dl*-propranolol having significant effects on either of these central measures.

E. Procedure

Each subject was informed in advance of the stress situations. This was necessary for ethical reasons and also because to reduce habituation on the second occasion it was advisable for subjects to know the exact nature of the experimental procedure. The elements of uncertainty and apprehension of the unknown, which commonly exist in normal and pathological anxiety, were

therefore excluded. Although this was to some extent unfortunate, it removed a source of variance in the results which would otherwise have been a problem. Subjects were shown the equipment and reassured that there were no dangers in any part of the experiment. Again, as in the first experiment, subjects with a history of cardiac disease or asthma were excluded but a test dose of propranolol was not given in advance. The stimulation of beta-agonist activity by the stressful procedures was expected to prevent the extreme bradycardia sometimes shown in sensitive individuals.

Testing was started at 09.45 hrs. a.m. and after completion of the first set of recordings at rest (about 25 minutes) an hour elapsed before the next experimental session. The remaining four test situations followed consecutively with only 5 minutes rest between each one. Testing was complete by 14.00 hrs. Subjects were allowed to eat a normal breakfast on the day of testing and asked to eat a similar meal on the second occasion of testing. To reduce familiarity with the test situations (and hence habituation) a clear month was required between the first (non-drug) occasion and the second (drug) occasion. The hour between first and second testings was necessary so that the drug could be absorbed and exert pharmacological effects during the remainder of the experiment. The drugs were given in three white capsules, each containing either placebo, diazepam (6 mg), *d*-propranolol (120 mg) or *d*-1 propranolol (120 mg) and were identical in appearance. They were taken immediately after the first testing at rest and subjects were asked to swallow them so that the taste of the drug was not noted.

This somewhat rigid procedure was adhered to throughout the experiment. There were two main reasons for this. The first was to compensate for diurnal effects which may be considerable for both physiological and psychological functions (Blake 1967; Colquohoun, 1969). The second was to ensure that the pharmacological effects of the drugs were a consequence of different pharmacological actions rather than time-related ones. The pharmacodynamics of the individual drugs are different; there are even differences between the plasma half-lives of *d*-propranolol and racemic propranolol (George, Fenyvesi, Conolly, and Dollery, 1972), but it was important to be certain that any variation shown in the recorded measures was free from contamination due to drugs being taken at different times. This was particularly necessary with the beta-adrenoceptor blocking agents as these act by competitive antagonism.

Not all the measures were recorded at each time of testing. The tapping and symbol copying tests were only given on the first, third, and fifth times so that practice effects were not too pronounced. Apart from these tests the other measures were recorded in the same order in each situation. The order followed was:

(*a*) finger tremor
(*b*) reaction-time task, including pulse rate, respiratory rate, and skin conductance

(*c*) tapping
(*d*) subjective mood scale
(*e*) bodily symptom scale
(*f*) symbol copying test.

After the end of the first stress situation (i.e. shocks alone) on the second occasion, 10 ml of venous blood was taken. An external observer who knew the code of the drugs transferred the blood to oxalate tubes for the propranolol samples and to sterile universal tubes for the diazepam samples. The placebo sample was discarded. 10–15 ml of venous blood from another person was taken on the same day as the propranolol samples and these were all stored at 4° C until analysed.

RESULTS

Analysis of variance was carried out on the change scores described earlier in this chapter. Each variable was analysed separately.

(1) Rating Scales

It was important to establish at the onset whether the test procedure was successful in inducing anxiety. In the present state of our knowledge the subject's self-ratings of anxiety are the most valid measures of this. Although it could be argued that the experiment deliberately led the subject to believe that he would be made anxious and that the changes in self-rating could be due to suggestion alone, the nature of the scales minimized this effect. The subjects were not to know that only the 'tense-relaxed' and 'calm-excited' scales were relevant in assessing anxiety and so they were more likely to give an unbiased rating of their feelings. To confirm that subjects did feel more anxious the factor ratings of anxiety were computed from the raw scales using the factor loadings described earlier [Chapter IV]. A one-way analysis of variance between the factor scores on each occasion confirmed that anxiety was induced by the stressful procedures to a highly significant degree. The differences between the mean ratings for the different stressful procedures were not significant but it is of interest that the phobic situation produced the most anxiety [Table 7].

It was also important to establish whether the distribution of data deviated n any way from a normal distribution and in this experiment the number of ratings was large enough to study this. The mood scale ratings approximated fairly well to a normal distribution, but those for the bodily symptom scales all showed a skewed distribution. The distribution of the mean scores is shown in Figure 12. Because of this the individual rating scores were all logged before analysis. It was also important to know whether the bodily feelings rated also showed an increase during the stressful procedures. Again using a one-way analysis of variance on the ratings for the first occasion it was

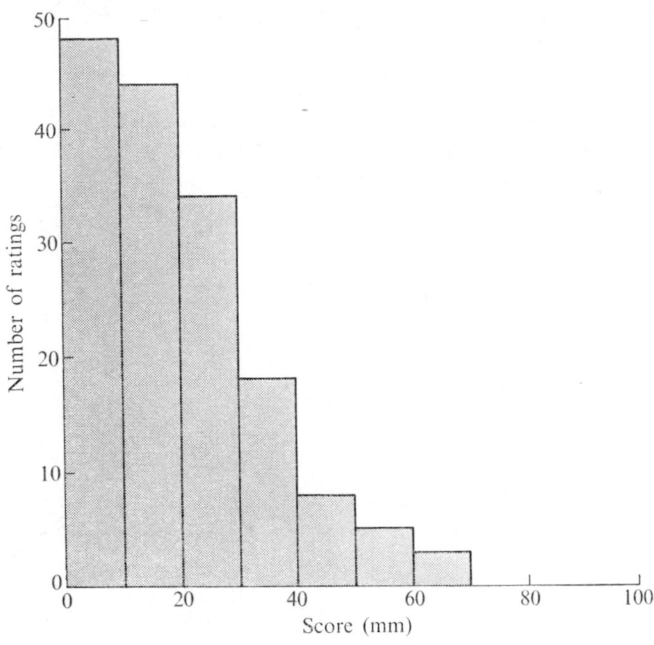

Figure 12

TABLE 7 ALTERATION IN MOOD AND BODILY SYMPTOMS DURING STRESS

		REST		SHOCKS ALONE		ISOPRENALINE + SHOCKS		PHOBIC STIMULUS		REST		F-RATIO (between times)
		mm	$\log_e$	mm	$\log_e$	mm	$\log_e$	mm	$\log_e$	mm	$\log_e$	
Mood factor	General factor (G)		20·6		20·5		21·4		20·2		22·1	2·7*
	Pleasure factor (P)		10·5		11·8		12·5		12·8		11·7	10·9†
	Anxiety factor (A)		4·8		5·8		5·9		6·1		5·0	19·1†
Bodily symptom	Sweating	21·5	3·07	51·2	3·94	45·6	3·82	41·1	3·72	21·5	3·07	20·6†
	Trembling	15·4	2·73	35·3	3·56	38·0	3·64	37·8	3·63	16·7	2·82	18·9†
	Palpitations	15·7	2·75	29·0	3·37	36·6	3·60	36·1	3·59	16·8	2·82	11·3†
	Nausea	2·4	0·88	6·7	1·90	11·4	2·43	10·9	2·38	6·2	1·82	6·2†
	Diarrhoea	4·3	1·46	2·4	0·88	2·8	1·03	3·6	1·28	3·0	1·10	1·0
	Urinary frequency	7·4	2·00	5·9	1·77	8·0	2·08	7·3	1·99	4·9	1·59	0·6
	Respiratory difficulty	8·8	2·17	12·8	2·55	23·8	3·17	21·1	3·05	13·9	2·63	7·3†
	Muscular tension	19·8	2·99	39·5	3·68	41·3	3·72	42·7	3·75	22·3	3·10	17·8†

* $p < 0·05$. † $p < 0·001$.

The mean scores for the thirty-two subjects are shown for the first occasion of testing only and are therefore free from drug effects.

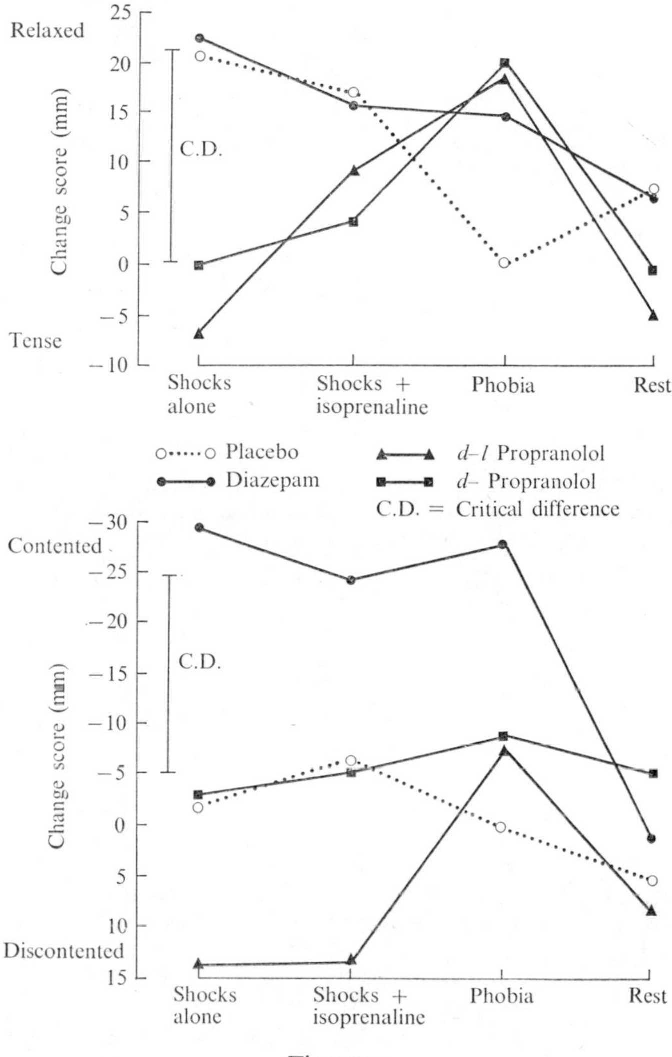

Figure 13

found that most of these feelings were more marked when the subjects were being stressed, although there were some important exceptions [TABLE 7].

Two of the subjective mood scales showed significant drug effects, the 'tense-relaxed' and 'contented-discontented' scales [FIG. 13]. In each instance diazepam was the most effective drug and racemic propranolol the least effective; these changes were most marked when the shocks were administered alone. As this part of the experiment took part $1\frac{1}{4}$–$1\frac{1}{2}$ hours after ingestion of the drug, at the time of peak sedation with diazepam and peak beta-blockade with propranolol, it is likely that the pharmacokinetics of the drug effects are more important than the nature of the stress in accounting for the results. It is of interest that the ratings recorded on the last occasion at rest show no drug differences, and perhaps the absence of stress at this time was

more relevant here. The scales were also converted to the three factors described in CHAPTER IV and analysed again. Only the anxiety factor showed significant drug effects, and these were only present on two of the times of testing [FIG. 14].

Only one of the bodily symptom scales showed significant drug effects; that indicating respiratory difficulty. Again diazepam was the most effective agent in reducing the symptoms and propranolol the least effective. The results of the ratings for all symptoms are shown in TABLE 8.

(2) PERFORMANCE AND PHYSIOLOGICAL TESTS

None of the three performance tests showed significant drug effects, nor was there any consistent trend. Diazepam, which might have been expected to produce some impairment of performance if it was given in too large a dose,

TABLE 8 DRUG EFFECTS ON SUBJECTIVE MOOD AND BODILY SYMPTOMS IN INDUCED ANXIETY

		F-RATIO (between drug groups)	F-RATIO (groups × times)
	Alert—drowsy	0·33	1·03
	Calm—excited	2·12	0·64
	Strong—feeble	1·18	1·32
	Muzzy—clear-headed	1·45	0·77
	Well co-ordinated—clumsy	0·96	0·49
	Lethargic—energetic	2·42	0·93
	Contented—discontented	3·31 *	2·07 *
	Troubled—tranquil	0·55	1·11
Mood Ratings	Slow—quick-witted	0·17	0·77
	Tense—relaxed	0·25	2·01 *
	Attentive—dreamy	1·59	1·77
	Incompetent—proficient	0·41	0·49
	Happy—sad	0·68	1·84
	Antagonistic—amicable	0·18	0·99
	Interested—bored	0·47	0·99
	Withdrawn—gregarious	1·27	1·42
Rating factors ($\log_e$ scores)	General factor (G)	0·74	0·60
	Pleasure factor (P)	1·91	0·80
	Anxiety factor (A)	1·06	2·03 *
	Sweating	0·78	0·25
	Trembling	0·65	0·40
Bodily Symptoms ($\log_e$ scores)	Palpitations	0·46	0·97
	Nausea	1·27	1·24
	Diarrhoea	0·35	1·41
	Urinary frequency	1·05	1·14
	Respiratory	3·52 *	0·24
	Muscular tension	2·27	1·07
	Mean total score	1·28	0·84

* $p < 0{\cdot}05$.

For 3 and 28 (drug groups) and 9 and 84 degrees of freedom (groups × times), F-ratios have to exceed 2·95 and 2·00 respectively to be significant at the 5 per cent level. For ease of presentation the mean change scores for each drug are not shown but details of these for significant F-ratios are shown in FIGURES 13 and 14.

did not in fact do so. These results confirm that the anti-anxiety effect of diazepam was not associated with a degree of sedation sufficient to affect performance.

Pulse rate was the only one of the physiological measures to show significant drug differences. Racemic propranolol led to a highly significant fall in pulse rate as expected, but dextropropranolol also produced a significant drop in pulse rate [FIG. 15]. As discussed earlier, dextro-propranolol has a small amount of beta-blocking activity of its own (Howe and Shanks, 1966; Barrett and Cullum, 1968) but this has never been shown to be of any relevance in human studies.

Tremor showed similar results to those in the first experiment with normal subjects [CHAPTER V]. There was a trend towards a reduction of tremor with

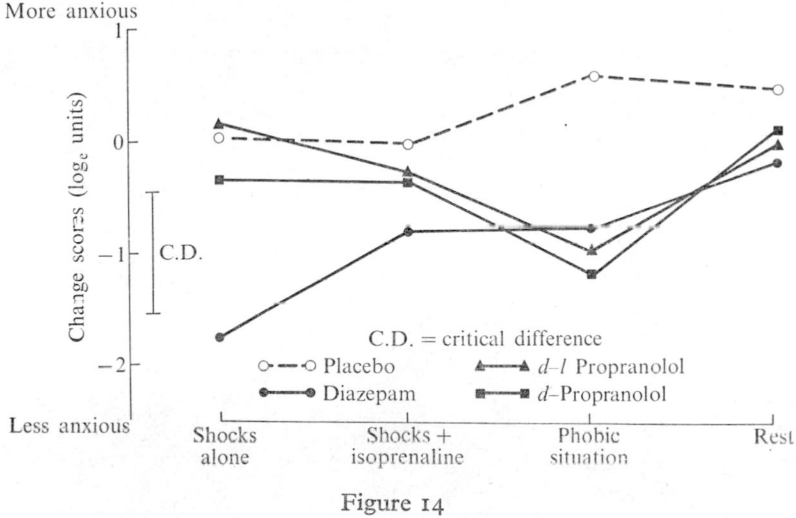

Figure 14

racemic propranolol but this did not reach significance for any tremor frequency. Respiratory rate showed some evidence of slowing with diazepam and although this was not significant it is consistent with the results of the appropriate bodily symptom scale. Skin conductance and fluctuations in skin conductance also showed no definite drug effects, although there was a tendency for conductance to be reduced with racemic propranolol, particularly after isoprenaline stimulation. Results of all the physiological measures and performance tests are shown in TABLE 9.

(3) PLASMA LEVELS

As in the first experiment, a wide variation was found in plasma levels of both isomers of propranolol. When these were correlated with the fall in pulse rate for each subject, again there was no apparent relationship in the group receiving racemic propranolol. In the dextro-propranolol group, however, there was such a relationship [TABLE 10]. Although the numbers are

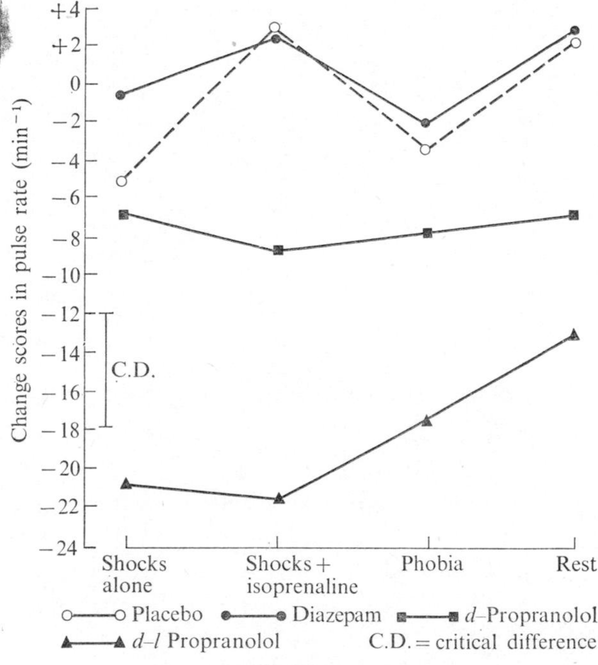

Figure 15

too small to assert this with any confidence, it appears that the small amount of beta-blockade that dextropropranolol possesses is related to the plasma level of the active substance and not to another metabolite. The metabolism of dextro-propranolol has not been studied in the same detail as the commercial racemic mixture but these results suggest it is unlikely that any of its metabolites have beta-blocking activity.

TABLE 9 DRUG EFFECTS ON PHYSIOLOGICAL MEASUREMENTS AND PERFORMANCE TESTS IN INDUCED ANXIETY

EXPERIMENTAL VARIABLES		F-RATIO (between drug groups)	F-RATIO (groups × times)
Physiological measures	Skin conductance	0·41	1·04
	Habituation of conductance	0·91	1·22
	Fluctuations in conductance	0·51	1·09
	Tremor (peak frequency) (Hz)	0·17	1·12
	Tremor (total amount) (finger acceleration) [2]	1·67	0·51
	Pulse Rate (beats/min.)	11·17 †	2·08 ‡
	Respiratory rate (beats/min.)	0·38	1·08
Performance tests	Reaction time	0·78	0·83
	Tapping *	1·02	1·35
	Symbol copying test *	0·15	1·89

* These measures were only taken three times on each occasion. † $p < 0{\cdot}001$. ‡ $p < 0{\cdot}05$.

For 3 and 28 (drug groups) and 9 and 84 degrees of freedom (groups × times), F-ratios have to exceed 2·95 and 2·00 respectively to be significant at the 5 per cent level. For ease of presentation the mean change scores for each drug are not shown but details of these for significant F-ratios are shown in FIGURE 18.

TABLE 10 CORRELATIONS BETWEEN PLASMA PROPRANOLOL LEVELS AND REDUCTION IN PULSE RATE DURING INDUCED ANXIETY

DRUG	SUBJECT NO.	SEX	REDUCTION IN PULSE RATE/MINUTE	PLASMA PROPRANOLOL LEVEL (μg/100 ML)
	1	M	10	19
	2	M	19·5	16
Racemic	3	M	11·5	12
Propranolol	4	F	10·5	13
	5	F	23	38
	6	F	17	7
	7	F	11	17·5
	8	M	43	12·5
	9	M	2	18
	10	F	9·5	12
	11	M	0	4
Dextro-	12	F	8·5	20
Propranolol	13	F	−3	3·5
	14	M	2	6
	15	M	5·5	8·5
	16	F	8	11

$r = 0{\cdot}061$ (racemic propranolol group)
$r = 0{\cdot}615$ (dextro-propranolol group)

The difference in pulse rate between the pre-drug and post-propranolol occasions during the first stress situation (shocks alone) was taken for correlation. The plasma sample was also taken at this time in the experiment.

SUMMARY

The results of this study show differences from the study just described with sotalol in anxious patients, and it seems likely that the pharmacological differences between propranolol and sotalol account for only a fraction of the disparity. Adequate beta-adrenoceptor blockade was achieved in the absence of sympathomimetic activity with both drugs and our earlier evidence suggested that the other properties of these compounds were not important in determining psychotropic effects. The psychological effects of racemic propranolol and its *d*-isomer on induced anxiety suggest that, at best, beta-adrenoceptor blockade has no effect on stress-induced anxiety and there are hints that it may have a negative anxiety-reinforcing effect from some of the mood changes [FIGS. 13 and 14].

Possible explanations for these generally negative findings include unsuitable recording methods (i.e. the data do not properly reflect what occurred in the experiment) and inadequate time for mood and associated changes to occur. On examination neither explanation carries much conviction. Although criticisms might be made of the applicability of the bodily symptom scale to studies with patients involving continuous administration of drugs these are not appropriate in a single dose study. The completion of a linear analogue scale at frequent intervals is ideal for detecting rapid changes and the analysis of bodily symptom ratings on the first occasion of testing [TABLE 7] showed

that the scales were sensitive to change. As for the second explanation, that the time involved was too short, it is difficult to see how the results would be altered over a longer period. Both diazepam and propranolol have short half-lives and show their major pharmacological effects within 2 hours of oral administration and their chronic effects show no qualitative differences from their acute ones.

It is more likely that there are inherent differences between induced anxiety (as created in this experiment) and the neurotic anxiety of psychiatric patients. To examine these more closely (and determine the therapeutic indications for beta-adrenoceptor blockade in morbid anxiety) another study was carried out in patients with chronic anxiety. The results of the studies already described, although contradictory, suggested a common theme; this needed testing.

CHAPTER VIII

DIFFERENTIAL EFFECTS OF BETA-ADRENOCEPTOR BLOCKADE IN SOMATIC AND PSYCHIC ANXIETY

DURING the trial of sotalol in chronic anxiety it was realized that clinical response was rarely related to a straightforward reduction in somatic symptoms. Examination of the group of patients that apparently responded to sotalol showed that they differed little in the dose of drug taken in the flexible regimen and in their physiological response as measured by reduction in finger tremor [TABLE 6]. Thus it appeared that the same pharmacological effect was perceived as beneficial by some patients but not by others. Such idiosyncrasy of response is hardly unusual in clinical trials, particularly so in psychiatry, but there did seem to be common features in the responder and non-responders. These features were not identified by any objective tests, so they had to be looked for elsewhere. The answer appeared to be hidden in the subjective experiences of the patients. Although direct evidence for these is obviously not possible there were sufficient indirect clues from the patients' own interpretation of their feelings to give a lead. One of the important factors in predicting improvement in the patients treated with sotalol appeared to be the nature of the main complaint. If the patient complained primarily of one or more bodily symptoms then he was more likely to get better with sotalol than if his symptoms were primarily of psychological disturbances associated with anxiety. This was only an impression and not in any way confirmed by the ratings carried out in the study. But this was hardly surprising; two patients may rate similarly on scales which measure bodily symptomatology and subjective anxiety yet conceal the information that one patient regards his bodily symptoms as paramount in contrast to the other who lays emphasis on his disturbed mood.

These differences are immediately recognisable by all those who have been involved in the care of patients with neurotic anxiety. It was decided to select a representative sample of patients from each of these types in the next study of beta-adrenoceptor blockade. One of the groups was delineated as somatically anxious, the other as psychically anxious. The distinction between them was based on the patients' own judgement of their symptoms at initial interview. In other respects it was hoped that they would be essentially similar, so that comparison between the two groups after treatment could be related to subjective interpretation alone. It will be noted that the distinction between somatic and psychic anxiety was not a simple one between patients with bodily symptoms and those without; it was the attitude of the patient towards

his symptoms that was the deciding factor. It would have been impossible to study this retrospectively from study of the ratings; the two groups had to be defined at the outset and studied prospectively.

Again it was decided to treat chronically anxious out-patients attending the Maudsley Hospital. The trial with sotalol had shown significant drug effects despite the comparatively small number of patients treated and only two of the forty measures had shown significant order effects, a finding which could have occurred by chance. A cross-over design was therefore chosen again, in which each patient took three drugs consecutively. The drugs chosen for comparison were racemic propranolol, diazepam, and placebo. The previous comparison of placebo and sotalol had yielded inconclusive results and an additional comparison with an established anxiety-reducing drug was felt to be necessary. To increase the number of patients available for study the criterion of six months duration of symptoms before first assessment was reduced to four months. To reduce the effects of spontanous improvement independent of the drug treatment each patient began treatment at least one week after initial assessment, the so-called 'washout' period (Feinstein, 1973). At initial assessment a full psychiatric history and examination was carried out and if patients had been chronically anxious in the absence of other affective changes they were considered for study. On the basis of subjective interpretation of symptoms patients were allocated to the somatic or psychic anxiety treatment group, if any. Just under half of the patients diagnosed as chronically anxious were not included in the study because they did not show clear-cut evidence of a primary emphasis on somatic or psychic symptoms. The twelve patients who completed the study are described in APPENDIX 1; from their description some idea of the separation of the two groups is obtained.

DESIGN

Each patient took racemic propranolol (40 mg), diazepam (2 mg) and placebo in flexible dosage for one week each. Each of the drugs has a short half-life (Shand *et al.*, 1970; van der Kleijn, 1971) and it was noted in the sotalol trial that clinical effects were noted in the first week of treatment if they were noted at all. Because of this a period of 1 week was thought to be adequate to detect drug effects. The order of treatment was determined by two Latin squares, one square for each treatment group. This ensured that any order effects of treatment, if present, would be fully compensated.

The drugs were made up in white capsules of identical appearance and a dosage range of one to three capsules three times daily was allowed. This allowed a maximum dosage of 360 mg daily for propranolol, so that if patients wished they could increase the dosage to a level at which central nervous system effects might be present. After each treatment the capsules were returned and the remainder counted. After each subject had received all three treatments he or she was asked to rank them in order of efficacy. In view

of the points discussed earlier only the subject's preference was recorded in this trial.

Psychological and Physiological Measures

It would have been ethically unjustifiable to cause stress in psychiatric patients who were already severely anxious. Because of this only a single short testing session took place at first assessment and after each treatment. On each occasion the same procedure was followed.

(1) The patient was assessed on the Hamilton Rating Scale for anxiety. The questions were asked in strict order so that anxiety, tension, and other psychic symptoms of anxiety were rated before the somatic symptoms. In this way unjustified deductions about the effect of somatic symptoms in reducing or increasing anxiety were avoided.

(2) A series of physiological measurements were recorded during the simple reaction time task [Chapter IV]. These measurements included skin conductance and its derivations, respiratory rate, finger tremor, and pulse rate. The electroencephalogram was also recorded and the results are described elsewhere (Tyrer and Lader 1974c). In addition reaction time and tapping speed were recorded. The patient then completed the subjective mood and bodily symptom scales before leaving the testing booth. A venous blood sample was then taken for estimation of plasma propranolol or serum diazepam. This was not always possible as some patients preferred not to have blood samples taken and such an investigation could not be justified on clinical grounds. The unused capsules of the drug he had just taken were returned and the patient supplied with a bottle containing the next drug (when indicated). The full sequence of investigations normally took about one hour.

The coding of the tablets was determined by an independent observer. Bottles of capsules were made up so that each contained sixty capsules of the appropriate drug, and these were labelled with a number. The mean dosage of capsules was calculated by subtracting the unused ones at the end of each treatment. The code was not broken until all twelve patients had completed the trial. To allow for possible sex differences in the symptoms of anxiety, the six patients in each treatment group were equally divided between the sexes.

Results

Fifteen patients entered the trial. The three drop-outs were all in the somatic group. One was unable to stop taking diazepam, a drug which she had been taking for two years before assessment. Another patient admitted towards the end of the trial that she had been taking other tablets, including benzodiazepines and barbiturates, as well as the prescribed tablets during the trial. The third patient failed to turn up for his last appointment after attend-

Of the points discussed earlier only the subject's expectancy was recorded in this trial.

PSYCHOLOGICAL AND PHYSIOLOGICAL MEASURES

It would have been clearly impracticable to carry out [illegible] in hospitalized patients who were already severely anxious. Because of this only a single short testing session took place at first assessment and after each treatment. On each occasion the same procedure was followed.

(i) The patient was [illegible] on the Hamilton [illegible]
The questionnaire [illegible]

[illegible]

Eleven patients completed the trial. The [illegible] sample group. One was unable to stop taking [illegible] had been taking for two years before treatment. Another [illegible] towards the end of the trial [illegible] had been taking [illegible] and [illegible] trial. The third patient failed to turn up for his last appointment [illegible]

ing the previous three. Analysis of data was therefore confined to the final group of twelve patients who completed the trial.

Dosage

The mean daily dosage of capsules taken for the twelve patients was placebo, 3·1; diazepam, 4·8 (9·6 mg) and propranolol, 3·0 (120 mg). The relatively low mean dose of propranolol suggests that no extra benefit was noted by patients who increased the dose as allowed in the flexible dose schedule. There was, however, a differential drug intake in the somatic and psychic anxiety groups with propranolol; a mean of 88 mg/day was taken in the psychic group, and 152 mg/day in the somatic one.

Subjective Preference

Diazepam was preferred to the other drugs by most of the patients. For seven of the patients it was a clear first choice, for four others an equal first choice and in only one instance was one of the other agents preferred [TABLE 11]. Propranolol appears to be no better than placebo if the group is taken as a whole, but when the somatic and psychic groups are recorded separately, it can be seen that a differential response is shown. The numbers in each cell are too small to permit adequate statistical analysis, but the results are suggestive of a real difference.

Ratings

Again parametric statistics were used to analyse the rating scores and other measures. Using a split-plot analysis of variance drug effects were estimated between groups and within subjects error variance. The F-ratios for drug effects and that for the drug-groups interaction were recorded separately. Thus any differential drug response between the two groups could be

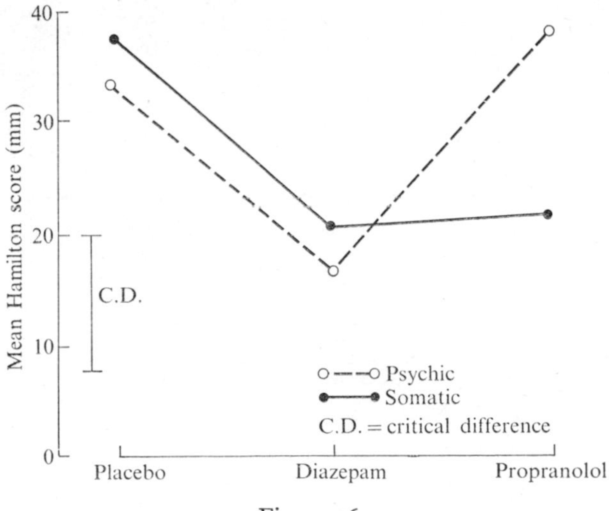

Figure 16

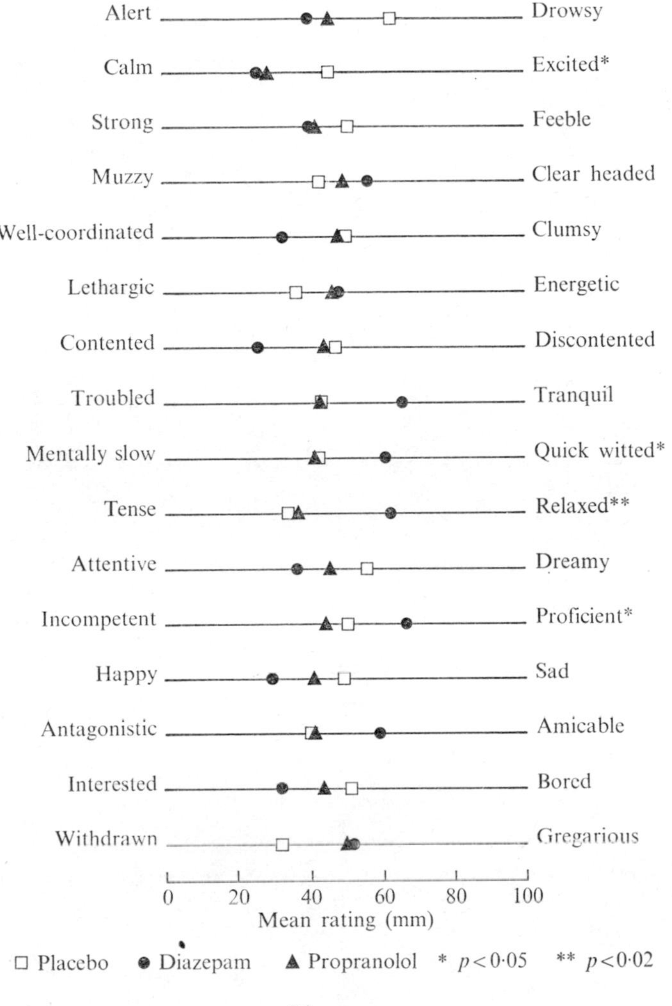

Figure 17

detected. For significant F-ratios Tukey's test was applied to calculate significant differences between pairs of means. The scores for the Hamilton ratings are shown in TABLE 12. Again it can be seen that diazepam is far superior to the other two drugs, significantly so on ten of the fifteen items comprising the Hamilton scale. A differential response between the two groups is shown on four of the ratings, however, and the mean total score also shows a differential drug response [FIG. 16]. The main contribution to this difference in response is shown in the ratings for somatic symptoms, particularly those for cardiovascular and respiratory ones.

The subjective mood ratings also confirmed the superiority of diazepam in improving feelings of well being [FIG. 17]. This also showed the anti-anxiety effect of diazepam, as both the ratings concerned with the factor of

anxiety discussed in CHAPTER IV showed significant drug differences. On this scale there was a trend towards a differential drug response but this only achieved significance on one of the rating scales, a finding which could have occurred by chance. However, in each case the trend was towards relatively better responses to diazepam in the psychic group and to propranolol in the somatic group.

The bodily symptom ratings reflected the findings on the other rating scales. Diazepam was superior on all ratings, even on those in which propranolol was clearly more effective in its physiological actions (e.g. pulse rate) [TABLE 13].

Physiological and performance measures

Neither skin conductance nor any of its derivations showed any drug effects which reached statistical significance. However, habituation did show a definite trend which almost reached significance. Both diazepam and propranolol increased habituation compared with placebo [TABLE 14].

There was a highly significant reduction in pulse rate with propranolol compared with diazepam and placebo [TABLE 14]. There was also a significant

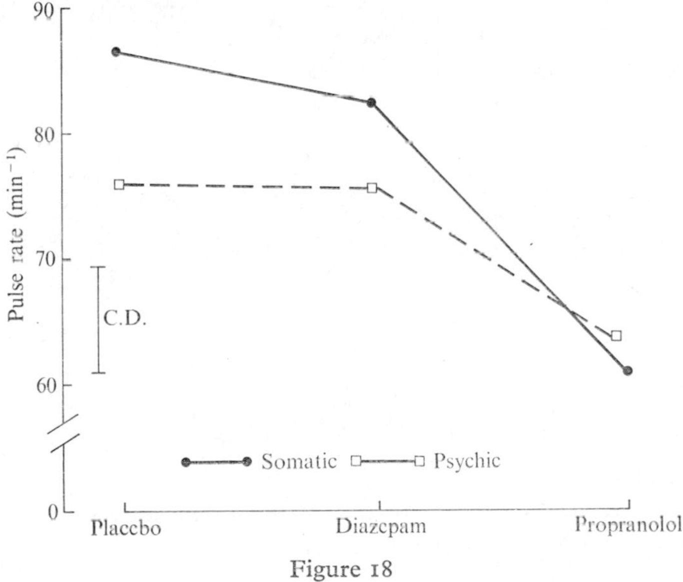

Figure 18

difference in the effect on pulse rate between the two treatment groups [FIG. 18]. The most likely reason for the latter finding is that the drug were not taken in equivalent dosage; a greater mean daily dose of propranolol was taken in the somatic group.

There were different effects of tremor at different frequencies. These are shown in FIGURE 19. Because of this the tremor at each of the individual frequencies was tested separately, and significant drug effects were shown at

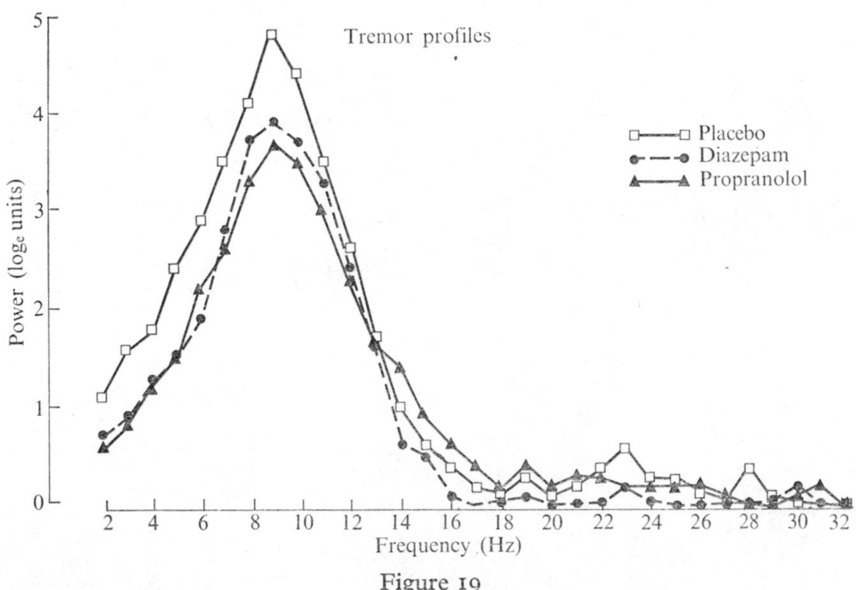

Figure 19

3, 5, 6, 7, 8, 9, and 10 Hz. At higher frequencies there were no significant drug effects, and this may be responsible for the lack of significant differences in total amount of tremor. Respiratory rate also showed no significant treatment differences although there was a trend towards an increased rate while taking placebo and a reduced one on propranolol [TABLE 14]. Neither tapping nor reaction time showed significant drug effects.

Plasma levels

Venous samples for analysis of propranolol were obtained from seven patients. The correlations between the plasma levels and reduction in pulse rate compared with placebo are shown [TABLE 15]. Again no clear relationship is apparent.

TABLE 11 PATIENTS' TREATMENT PREFERENCES

		RANK ORDER (WITH CORRECTION FOR TIED RANKS)		
GROUP	CASE NO.	Diazepam	Propranolol	Placebo
Somatic	1	1	2	3
	2	1	2	3
	3	2	2	2
	4	2	1	3
	5	1	2	3
	6	1·5	1·5	3
Psychic	1	1	3	2
	2	1	2	3
	3	1	3	2
	4	1	3	2
	5	1·5	3	1·5
	6	1	3	2

Kendall's coefficient of concordance (w) (Siegel, 1956) $= 0{\cdot}51$; $p < 0{\cdot}01$.

TABLE 12 MEAN HAMILTON RATING SCORES FOR SOMATIC AND PSYCHIC ANXIETY GROUPS, WITH EACH DRUG TREATMENT

		MEAN RATING (0–100 mm)							
		Placebo		Diazepam		Propranolol		F-RATIO between drugs	F-RATIO (drugs × groups)
		Somatic	Psychic	Somatic	Psychic	Somatic	Psychic		
Psychic Symptoms	Anxiety	53·5	51·8	32·3	26·0	37·8	53·8	8·3*	2·0
	Tension	56·8	50·7	31·5	30·7	43·2	55·0	5·9†	0·9
	Fears	40·8	33·7	25·3	28·3	21·7	36·8	2·6	2·7
	Insomnia	21·3	23·2	8·2	2·7	20·8	26·0	10·0*	0·7
	Intellectual	32·2	24·2	13·3	11·2	11·5	31·2	4·1‡	3·4
	Behaviour at interview	53·2	45·3	32·5	28·0	33·5	54·2	9·0*	5·7†
	Depression	22·7	22·0	12·2	8·3	25·3	28·3	4·4‡	0·2
Somatic Symptoms	Somatic Muscular	19·2	33·0	11·2	12·8	9·0	25·2	2·9	0·9
	Somatic Sensory	31·5	27·5	15·5	11·5	19·2	28·5	2·2	0·5
	Cardiovascular	41·8	34·0	19·0	23·7	8·3	51·5	3·3	8·6*
	Respiratory	33·7	29·5	26·3	7·5	20·5	38·7	5·5†	7·6*
	Gastro-intestinal	31·3	21·2	13·0	9·3	13·8	30·8	4·3†	3·5
	Genito-urinary	23·3	21·0	15·8	4·7	10·3	12·2	4.8†	1·2
	Autonomic	40·5	34·7	23·8	19·8	19·7	41·5	2·6	2·5
	Behaviour physiological	56·7	44·7	33·0	28·5	29·0	49·2	9·1*	6·4*
	Mean total score	37·2	33·1	20·9	16·8	21·6	37·5	10·2*	5·0†

* $p < 0{\cdot}01$. † $p < 0{\cdot}025$. ‡ $p < 0{\cdot}05$.

TABLE 13 MEAN BODILY SYMPTOM RATINGS FOR SOMATIC AND PSYCHIC ANXIETY GROUPS WITH EACH DRUG TREATMENT

	MEAN RATING (0–100 mm) ($\log_e$ units)							
	Placebo		Diazepam		Propranolol		F-RATIO between drugs	F-RATIO (drugs × groups)
BODILY SYMPTOM	Somatic	Psychic	Somatic	Psychic	Somatic	Psychic		
Sweating	3·5	2·0	2·5	1·0	2·7	1·0	4·4*	0·0
Trembling	3·4	2·2	1·9	1·0	2·1	2·4	5·7†	1·7
Palpitations	3·2	2·4	2·1	1·8	1·9	2·7	1·6	1·6
Nausea	3·0	2·1	1·2	0·5	1·0	2·2	11·8‡	5·3†
Diarrhoea	1·9	2·0	0·7	0·8	0·7	2·5	4·4*	2·7
Urinary frequency	2·1	2·6	0·6	0·9	1·4	2·6	8·3‡	0·6
Respiratory difficulty	3·3	2·6	2·5	1·0	2·4	3·2	3·3	2·5
Muscular tension	3·6	2·3	2·5	1·7	2·6	2·4	1·4	0·6
Mean total	3·0	2·3	1·8	1·1	1·9	2·4	9·0‡	2·9

* $p < 0{\cdot}05$. † $p < 0{\cdot}025$. ‡ $p < 0{\cdot}01$.

TABLE 14 PHYSIOLOGICAL RESPONSES TO PLACEBO, PROPRANOLOL AND DIAZEPAM IN SOMATIC AND PSYCHIC ANXIETY GROUPS

		PLACEBO		DIAZEPAM		PROPRANOLOL		F-RATIO	F-RATIO
EXPERIMENTAL VARIABLE	UNITS	Somatic	Psychic	Somatic	Psychic	Somatic	Psychic	between drugs	(drugs × groups)
Skin conductance	log μmhos	14·1	7·8	9·4	8·3	7·7	7·0	1·4	1·1
Habituation in skin conductance	change in log μmhos	0·05	0·00	− 0·04	− 0·03	− 0·03	− 0·03	3·4	0·9
Fluctuations in skin conductance	number/min.	3·3	2·9	3·1	2·5	2·4	2·7	0·5	0·4
Tremor (2–32 Hz)	$\log_e$ units	6·2	5·8	5·7	5·7	5·3	5·3	2·0	0·1
Tremor (frequency of main peak)	Hz	9·25	8·5	9·25	8·5	9·6	8·6	1·3	0·6
Tremor (amount at main peak)	$\log_e$ units	5·8	5·0	4·9	4·7	4·1	4·6	4·3*	1·6
Respiratory rate	breaths/min.	20·6	18·5	18·6	18·8	18·8	17·4	2·7	1·8
Pulse rate	beats/min.	86·5	76·0	82·5	75·5	60·9	63·5	38·2*	4·1

* $p < 0{\cdot}001$. † $p < 0{\cdot}05$.

TABLE 15 CORRELATION BETWEEN PLASMA PROPRANOLOL LEVELS AND REDUCTION IN PULSE RATE

PATIENT NO.	REDUCTION IN PULSE RATE/MINUTE	PLASMA PROPRANOLOL LEVEL (μg/100 ML)
1	19	56
3	15·5	16
5	34·5	5
6	21·5	10·5
8	11·0	3·5
9	41	16
12	43·5	5·5

Correlation coefficient (r) = −0·242

The values for the reduction in pulse rate are taken as the difference between the pulse rate when on placebo compared with that on propranolol.

Discussion of these results is best considered in comparison with those of the early experiments. Although the number of patients in the somatic and psychic anxiety groups was small there were marked differences in their response to the three drugs. Before coming to any conclusions about the significance of these differences it was important to make sure that influences distinct from somatic or psychic interpretations of symptoms were not responsible for the findings. In particular it was possible that the somatic and psychic groups merely differed in the degree of their anxiety. The greater the anxiety the more marked the somatic symptoms and it could be argued that the patients' emphasis on somatic or psychic aetiology was a function of this. The results of the ratings on the first occasion of testing (i.e. before any drug was prescribed) were therefore analysed (by a one-way analysis of variance). Only two of the variables showed significant differences at the 5 per cent level (reaction time and tapping), a finding which could equally occur by chance. What is more, the somatic symptoms experienced by the patients during the study showed no consistent group differences; if degree of symptomatology was the true distinguishing factor between the groups such differences should have merged. Diagnostic differences between the two groups were also small. All patients had generalized anxiety and although more patients had experienced phobic symptoms in the psychic anxiety group than in the somatic one [APPENDIX 1] there was no evidence that this contributed to clinical response. Sex differences were compensated for by having equal sex representation in the groups and age was the only other demographic variable to differ: the somatically anxious patients (mean age 28·2 years) were younger than the psychically anxious ones (mean age 38·2 years). It is possible that somatic symptoms may be the primary complaint in the younger anxious patients more often than in the older ones but it is unlikely that age itself could account for the differences in drug response shown in the study.

The differences therefore appear to be related to the distinction already made between somatic and psychic anxiety. Can this distinction explain why

(i) diazepam is superior to propranolol and placebo in relieving both bodily symptoms and anxious mood in both somatic and psychic anxiety?

(ii) despite little *physiological* difference between the physiological effects of propranolol in somatic and psychic anxiety there are marked *psychological* differences in its effects in the two groups?

At first glance these findings seem contradictory. If the somatic-psychic distinction has no bearing on clinical response to diazepam why should it be relevant in determining response to propranolol? The results shown in TABLES 13 and 14 illustrate that the reduction in bodily symptoms with diazepam is not accompanied by reduction in measured physiological effects so it is curious that propranolol, presumably by altering peripheral physiological responses, does affect subjective feelings. Perhaps the findings are best explained by analogy. If anxiety is regarded as a stream, continuously being replenished and discharged (like the original Freudian concept of libido) the sourse is at a central level and the outflow at a peripheral level in the form of symptoms. Diazepam dams the flow near the source so that all symptoms, both psychic and somatic, are relieved. Propranolol dams part of the flow near its end, when it has already divided into tributaries, and so it is hardly surprising that it is less effective than diazepam. (Leading from this analogy it is worth emphasizing that neither treatment actually stops the flow at source—a point which critics of pharmacotherapy have frequently used in defence of alternative approaches.)

Even this analogy does not explain the difference between somatic and psychic anxiety response to propranolol. To extend the analogy further and postulate that the larger mean dose of propranolol in the somatic anxiety group dams more of the stream than the smaller dose in the psychic group does not seem to be justified from the other experimental results. These give no evidence for a dose-related response to beta-adrenoceptor blockade in the therapeutic range. As a flexible dosage regimen was used the difference in drug intake is probably best explained by the response after first taking the drug—patients take more if they feel better. There needed to be a better explanation for the findings than the influences of dosage and demographic differences; the relationship between physiological responses and subjective experience of them seemed to be at the heart of the matter.

CHAPTER IX

RELATIONSHIP BETWEEN PERIPHERAL PHYSIOLOGICAL CHANGES AND SUBJECTIVE MOOD IN ANXIETY

IF, as the evidence from these and other studies suggests, propranolol and other beta-adrenoceptor blocking drugs produce any clinical benefit they may possess in anxiety by peripheral blockade, the process of events following drug absorption must involve conscious or unconscious awareness of physiological changes.

blockade of beta-receptors	→	altered function of physiological processes	→	conscious or unconscious awareness of altered function	→	subjective relief

The alteration in physiological functions following beta-blockade may be represented by the changes in the psychophysiological measurements used in these studies and the ratings of bodily feelings are a measurement of conscious awareness of such physiological changes. If *conscious* awareness of these changes is necessary for relief of anxiety then there should be a close relationship between bodily symptoms and physiological measurements, but if this appreciation of change occurs unconsciously a poor relationship would be shown.

The extent of this relationship was therefore examined in different forms of anxiety. Product-moment correlation co-efficients were calculated between bodily symptom rating and the corresponding physiological measurement in each subject on a number of occasions under different external conditions. The within-subject correlations were then combined (using Fisher's z-transformation) to give a weighted mean correlation co-efficient for the total sample. If the individual correlations were homogeneous (using a chi-squared test (Edwards, 1965)) it was statistically justified to regard the weighted correlation coefficient as representative of the whole sample. This method of assessing the relationship was used because the relationship between symptoms and physiological function within subjects was felt to be preferable to that between subjects. It has already been noted that analogue scales are best used to measure change; the exact position of a mark on a 10 cm line is hardly an absolute measurement. The measurement of within-subject correlations also avoids variation due to individual response specificity.

Initially the relationship was measured in a group of sixteen normal subjects who were taking part in a study of diurnal variation in physiological tremor (Tyrer and Bond, 1974). Subjects were tested hourly for 8 hours

during the course of a normal working day. Finger tremor was measured as described earlier [CHAPTER IV] and on each occasion subjects rated themselves for the bodily symptom rating of tremor [FIG. 3] and the mood rating scales of tension and anxiety [FIG. 2]. The rating scores were logged to correct for a skewed distribution and then correlated with tremor at different frequencies. The results showed a small but consistent relationship between tremor rating and physiological tremor at lower frequencies [TABLE 16].

TABLE 16 CORRELATIONS BETWEEN TREMOR ACTIVITY AT DIFFERENT FREQUENCIES AND SELF-RATINGS

TREMOR FREQUENCY (c/sec)	SELF-RATINGS		
	Tremor	Anxiety	Tension
2– 5	0·267*	0·164	0·037
6– 9	0·234†	0·275‡	0·144
10–13	0·227†	−0·124	−0·050
14–17	0·198	−0·002	−0·075
2–32 (total)	0·249*	0·177	0·057
Peak frequency	0·344‡	0·101	0·076

* $p < 0·02$. † $p < 0·05$. ‡ $p < 0·01$.

Normal subjects at rest therefore have some awareness of at least one psychophysiological function but the relationship is not a close one. These subjects were tested at rest and their tremor was not pathological, so the relationship was again examined in induced anxiety in normal subjects. The symptom ratings and physiological measurements described in CHAPTER VII were employed. Thus the four measurements of pulse and respiratory rate, tremor and skin conductance were correlated with the corresponding bodily symptoms for each of the thirty-two subjects. These correlations were measured for recordings taken on the first five times of testing (i.e. before any drug was given) and converted to a weighted mean correlation. The results are shown in TABLE 17.

In the final study of propranolol and diazepam in chronic anxiety [CHAPTER VIII] correlations were estimated for the same four bodily symptoms and psychophysiological measurements. The recordings taken at first assessment and after each drug were included. These correlations differed from those of the other studies in that the interval between measurements was a week and not just a few hours, and that the physiological changes were greater because of drug effects.

The results suggest that in normal and induced anxiety the relationship between bodily feelings and physiological change is a consistent one but of a low order. In psychic anxiety the relationship is similar but in somatic anxiety a much stronger association exists between symptoms and physiological events. It therefore appears that the somatically orientated patient has greater awareness of physiological changes and that such bodily symptoms as he has are correct reflections of autonomic (and somatic) function. This

conclusion could only be tentative as the correlations were calculated on only four occasions for each subject and measurements were made at weekly intervals.

A separate investigation was therefore made into the inter-relationship between anxiety, the bodily symptom of 'fast-beating heart' and pulse rate in somatic and psychic anxiety (Tyrer, 1975). In-patients and out-patients were considered for the study if their primary diagnosis was felt to be either a chronic anxiety state or a 'functional disorder'. Many of the patients seen were referred from medical departments of the Southampton University

TABLE 17 WEIGHTED MEAN CORRELATIONS BETWEEN PULSE RATE AND SUBJECTIVE RATINGS

	CORRELATION WITH PULSE RATE (R)	
RATING	Somatic (n = 108)	Psychic (n = 72)
Relaxed—tense	(0·54*) n.h.	0·26†
Anxious—calm	−0·46*	−0·22
Heart rate	(0·48*) n.h.	0·20
Palpitations	0·35*	0·26†

* $p < 0{\cdot}001$. † $p < 0{\cdot}05$. n.h. = total sample not homogeneous.

The correlations in brackets are those for the occasions on placebo (relaxed-tense) and propranolol (heart rate) which were homogeneous.

Hospitals and differed from the patients previously seen at the Maudsley Hospital in that they complained only of physical symptoms and denied psychological complaints. For reasons discussed later these patients were felt to constitute an extreme form of somatic anxiety and were therefore included in the study. Patients considered suitable for the study were seen on two separate occasions, at least 24 hours apart. They had not been taking any psychotropic drugs for at least a week before testing. On each occasion patients took 20 mg of racemic propranolol or placebo tablets of identical appearance under double-blind conditions. Their radial pulse rate was recorded (by a nurse) at ten minute intervals for 90 minutes after taking the tablets and each time the pulse rate was recorded patients rated themselves on analogue scales for anxiety, their subjective awareness of heart rate and palpitations [FIG. 20]. The latter two ratings were recorded separately as anxious palpitations may occur in the absence of tachycardia (Bonn *et al.*, 1972).

The patients were separated in somatic and psychic anxiety groups as described earlier. Ten patients were studied, six with somatic and four with psychic anxiety, the main clinical features of these are described in APPENDIX 2. The results were not evaluated until all the patients had finished the study. The code was then broken and the correlations between pulse rate and subjective ratings calculated. Again the correlations were consistent with those of the earlier study. High correlations were found between pulse rate and self-ratings in the somatic anxiety group of patients and low correlations in those with psychic anxiety. These differences were not confined to the ratings of

[illegible]

[illegible] in [illegible]

1. Please rate the way you feel for each of the following.

2. Regard the line as representing the full range for each feeling.

3. Rate your feelings as they are at present.

4. Mark perpendicularly across each line.

Date: A.M.

P.M.

RELAXED ______________________________ TENSE

ANXIOUS ______________________________ CALM

How fast do you think your heart is beating at present.

VERY SLOW ______________________________ VERY FAST

Have you any palpitations at present?

NONE ______________________________ MANY

Figure 20

bodily symptoms alone. Significant correlations between subjective ratings of anxiety and pulse rate were also found in somatic but not in psychic anxiety [TABLE 18].

The results of all these studies suggest that somatic anxiety is different from psychic, induced, and normal anxiety. In the latter conditions, bodily feelings are a pale reflection of the physiological changes occurring, and so

TABLE 18 CORRELATIONS BETWEEN BODILY SYMPTOM RATINGS AND PHYSIOLOGICAL MEASUREMENTS IN INDUCED, SOMATIC, AND PSYCHIC ANXIETY

BODILY SYMPTOM	PHYSIOLOGICAL MEASUREMENT	INDUCED ANXIETY (n = 96)	SOMATIC ANXIETY (n = 12)	PSYCHIC ANXIETY (n = 12)
Sweating	Skin conductance	n.h.	−0·13	+0·04
Tachycardia and palpitations	Pulse rate	+0·35*	+0·70‡	−0·10
Trembling	Tremor (2–5 Hz)	+0·15	+0·80‡	+0·46
Trembling	Tremor (6–9 Hz)	+0·35*	+0·77‡	−0·05
Trembling	Tremor (10–13 Hz)	+0·21†	+0·90‡	+0·43
Difficulty in breathing	Respiratory rate	+0·31‡	+0·78‡	−0·46

* $p < 0{\cdot}001$. † $p < 0{\cdot}05$. ‡ $p < 0{\cdot}01$. n.h. = not homogeneous.

it is likely that they are secondary to altered mood rather than direct awareness of peripheral changes. When the subject becomes anxious he rates himself as having the appropriate increase of bodily feelings (presumably through prior learning that such symptoms are increased in anxiety) even though these changes are not occurring at a peripheral physiological level. In somatic anxiety, on the other hand, the peripheral changes are perceived correctly and as anxiety also correlates well with these changes it is more likely that subjective anxiety is to some extent dependent on peripheral changes. As alteration of mood occurs with peripheral beta-adrenoceptor blockade in such subjects this dependence appears to be important and not just a fleeting relationship which can quickly change. In somatic anxiety it does not seem to matter much which physiological system is most active in eliciting bodily feelings. If there is an increase of awareness of one aspect of bodily symptomatology then it appears to generalise to other physiological systems; the patient with a functional cardiovascular disorder perceives not only his pulse rate correctly but also his trembling and respiratory rate. The lack of any relationship with sweating may be a true representation but could also be an artefact. When repeat measurements of palmar sweat gland activity are taken at different times under differing external conditions of temperature and humidity then changes can occur independently of anxiety and these may be greater than effects due to mood change.

Why should there be this difference in somatic and psychic anxiety? What is happening to increase a subject's awareness of his bodily function? Was William James at least partly right when he maintained that visceral changes were the cause of emotion? All these questions come to mind when considering the implication of these results, and will be dealt with in the final chapter.

CHAPTER X

CONCLUSIONS

As psychopharmacology and psychophysiology frequently yield a surfeit of data, and as this may have been a problem encountered by the reader in the previous chapters, it is appropriate at this stage to list the main findings again. These are confined to results which show constancy in all the studies described and are therefore more likely to lend themselves to general conclusions.

(1) Pharmacological blockade of beta-adrenergic receptors is an appropriate method of examining the relationship between bodily and psychological feelings in anxiety. At most doses within the therapeutic range no evidence of central nervous system effects is found.

(2) The effects of anxiety on the cardiovascular system and on physiological tremor are attenuated by beta-adrenoceptor blockade but sweat gland activity and respiratory rate are not significantly altered.

(3) Beta-adrenoceptor blocking agents produce similar physiological changes in normal subjects at rest and during induced anxiety, and in psychiatric patients with morbid anxiety.

(4) Bodily feelings (including those relating to the cardiovascular system and tremor) are also increased in all forms of anxiety.

The first question asked at the beginning of this series of investigations was whether beta-adrenoceptor blockade was an appropriate method of studying the relationship between subjective anxiety and bodily feelings. The results give qualified assent; the method is appropriate but can only confine itself to a part of bodily symptomatology in anxiety. Symptoms which are related to activity in physiological systems unaffected by beta-blockade cannot be included, although they are valuable for comparison.

The second question was whether bodily feelings are important in the genesis and maintenance of anxiety. At one level this is unanswerable. The experience of anxiety is subjective and cannot be measured. Whether this experience occurs immediately before or immediately after bodily changes in anxiety cannot be determined, and all methods of investigating the matter have to measure variables which are several steps removed from these primary events. Beta-adrenoceptor blockade is one of several methods which can be used; by altering bodily feelings reversibly without producing central action interpretations can be made about the practical importance of bodily feelings in anxiety. They do not tell us whether mood or bodily changes occur first

in the genesis of anxiety. Where both are present they can interact in countless ways and obscure the original events. We are on firmer ground when discussing factors involved in the maintenance of anxiety. How bodily feelings and mood interact can be studied by modifying one state while measuring the other and beta-adrenoceptor blocking drugs satisfy this criterion. Any explanation of the interaction and the role of bodily feelings in anxiety has to account for the following facts:

(1) In normal (and induced) anxiety bodily feelings are more pronounced than when the subject is calm. They do not correlate well with the peripheral physiological changes occurring in anxiety and alteration of the physiological effects by pharmacological blockade produces little subjective mood or bodily feeling changes.

(2) In morbidly anxious subjects who primarily complain of psychological symptoms bodily feelings are increased but, as in normal anxiety, they correlate poorly with physiological changes and are unaffected by pharmacological blockade.

(3) In morbidly anxious subjects who primarily complain of somatic symptoms bodily feelings are increased and correlate highly with physiological changes. When the physiological effects are altered by peripheral pharmacological blockade there is a corresponding reduction in bodily symptoms accompanied by an improvement in subjective anxiety.

The differential effects of beta-blockade in normal persons and in the morbidly anxious with psychological and somatic symptoms can be explained in several ways. Firstly, if bodily symptoms are minor, drug effects on them are more difficult to discern. The relationship between bodily feelings and physiological changes would also be very weak. Secondly, anxious patients with marked somatic symptoms may have undergone a secondary conditioning procedure in that their awareness or bodily symptoms becomes associated with the feelings of subjective anxiety. A high correlation between them would develop, and blockade of the peripheral physiological changes would be associated with a drop in feelings of anxiety. Thirdly, it is possible that symptom mechanisms in patients with somatic anxiety are different in nature from those of patients with psychological symptoms of anxiety. The negative findings of other workers with beta-adrenoceptor blocking drugs in induced anxiety corroborate these results (Eliasch *et al.*, 1967; Holmberg *et al.*, 1967; Cleghorn *et al.*, 1970). The only study in which beta-blockade has been reported to produce improvement in anxiety in normal subjects is that by Stone and his colleagues (Stone, Gleser, and Gottschalk, 1973; Gottschalk, Stone, and Gleser, 1974). Volunteers were treated with 60 mg of propranolol or placebo in three divided doses in the 12 hours preceding testing. The results suggested that at initial testing the group receiving propranolol were significantly less anxious, but that these differences disappeared when the subjects were stressed. Since the subjects were not tested before the adminis-

tration of propranolol and placebo the differences at the first testing might have been chance findings independent of beta-adrenoceptor blockade, and so the authors' emphasis on differential response in basal and induced anxiety may be misplaced. The results of beta-blockade in normal subjects at rest reported earlier [CHAPTER V] do not support any suggestion of an anti-anxiety effect in this group.

There is much greater support for anti-anxiety effects in morbidly anxious patients. The evidence has been summarized earlier [CHAPTER II] and in addition to studies in anxious patients there is strong evidence that beta-adrenoceptor blockade is effective in functional cardiovascular disorders (Marsden, 1971). One recent well-controlled trial showed no evidence that propranolol had any anxiety-reducing effects in morbid anxiety (Ramsay, Greer, and Bagley, 1973) but as the selection criteria were such that patients with psychic anxiety were likely to predominate this result is not unexpected.

The division of anxiety into somatic and psychic categories was felt to be the best way of separating the responders and non-responders to beta-blockade. As stated earlier [CHAPTER VIII] the separation of these groups was based on subjective interpretation of the prime symptoms rather than their severity. Although the limitations of any categorisation based on subjective report are acknowledged, the separation of psychic and somatic anxiety is a plausible one and is recognizable by observers as well as through subjective account.

Why should this division exist in the interpretation of the symptoms of anxiety? The variation in the symptomatology of morbid anxiety is much greater than in normal anxiety and unlikely to be explained merely in terms of degree. There are many psychodynamic interpretations of bodily symptoms in anxiety. Some are based on the early concept of symptom substitution (Freud, 1949); the subject is unable to admit to himself the real cause of his anxiety and escapes from the dilemma by substituting a physical symptom, which distracts attention from the fundamental origins of the conflict and brings temporary relief. The vicissitudes of the primary (psychic) conflict may be reflected in the way symptoms are described, hence the term, 'organ jargon' (Adler, 1917). This 'explanation' of bodily symptomatology in emotional states would be more satisfactory if it did not describe symptoms which are physiologically understandable without further elaboration. No clear evidence of symptom substitution has been shown after symptomatic therapy and the concept is an over-simplified one (Crisp, 1966).

Another explanation is that invoked by Richter (1940) and Breggin (1964) described earlier [CHAPTER II]. The concept of feedback is central to their view. When anxiety occurs (for whatever reason) the bodily symptoms accompanying it may trigger further attacks of anxiety even after the original anxiety stimulus had disappeared. The positive feed-back loop of anxiety → bodily symptoms → further anxiety can therefore become self-perpetuating. It could be argued that the difference between the somatic and psychic

anxiety patient is in the strength of the learned association between bodily feelings and anxiety. However, it fails to account for the symptoms of the patient who denies all subjective anxiety and complains only of its bodily manifestations.

The explanation of these differences which is most consistent with the experimental findings of these studies is outlined elsewhere (Tyrer, 1973). In the first chapter more emphasis was laid on the James–Lange hypothesis of emotion than on other currently more acceptable theories. This was because this hypothesis does give prominence to the physiological changes in emotion although the order of events is probably wrong. As the James–Lange hypothesis deals with subjective phenomena it cannot be examined directly using scientific methods. Accordingly, it cannot be refuted and its usefulness is confined to providing philosophical insights into how emotions might be engendered. Undoubtedly, sensations play an important part in shaping the form of emotional experience (Richter, 1940; Schachter and Singer, 1962; Breggin, 1964; Valins and Ray, 1967), but their precise role is not established.

It appears that although bodily feelings occur during emotional changes in the normal subject, they are generally minor in significance.

However, when we consider the clinical aspects of morbid anxiety bodily symptoms often assume much greater importance than in normal anxiety. These symptoms often dominate the patient's account of his condition, occasionally to the extent that the symptoms alone constitute the complaint and subjective emotional changes are denied. Every clinician, no matter in which speciality he practises, has encountered such patients. For want of a better term, their complaints are described as 'functional', (a paradoxical term since it is not clear what function such complaints serve) and they occupy the hinterland between psychiatry and medicine, seeking a foothold in both specialities but finding haven in neither. They do not even have the status of the patient with a psychosomatic illness, in whom there is a demonstrable disease process, whatever its aetiology. The patients whom Freud described as having 'anxiety equivalents' (1894) fall into this category. Such patients have been studied in detail by Misch (1935), who, although approaching the subject from a psychodynamic viewpoint, still concluded that 'primarily neurotic anxiety states which are isolated from external psychical influence should be treated in a somatic manner'.

Can these differences in the clinical presentation of anxiety be explained by different levels of awareness of the stimulus producing the mood change. Thus:

In normal emotion the subject recognises the provoking stimulus, usually an external one, which gives rise to the emotion. He experiences the somatic feelings of physiological arousal, but as he has already detected the source of arousal he regards these as secondary phenomena. In morbid emotion the subject may or may not recognise the provoking stimulus. He is particularly prone to ignorance if the stimulus is an internal psychic one. If he fails to recognise it, the bodily feelings that he

experiences are not understood. He is therefore likely to look upon these as primary phenomena and deny the psychic aspects of his condition. Further exposure to the stimulus tends to reinforce the initial interpretation of the feelings experienced.

An example of the first group is the patient with a dog phobia who is fully aware of the cause of his fear and will therefore not attach much importance to his symptoms, whereas the patient who experiences an acute attack of panic while at rest may infer a somatic cause of the attack and regard his anxiety as secondary. The above-mentioned theory accounts for the differences in symptomatology between three groups:

(*a*) Normal subjects who become anxious under stress but always relate their symptoms to the stress and therefore seldom complain of bodily symptoms.

(*b*) Patients with 'neurotic' disorders, who constitute a continuum; at one extreme psychic symptoms are complained of entirely and bodily feelings disregarded, and at the other extreme bodily symptoms dominate the clinical picture. Even in the latter group symptoms of anxiety are noted although the subject may attribute them primarily to concern over his somatic complaint.

(*c*) Patients with 'functional' disorders, who are aware only of their bodily symptoms and therefore infer that these symptoms have an organic cause. Psychic symptoms are often denied altogether and the patient is more likely to attend a general medical than a psychiatric clinic. Emotional stresses in such individuals lead to further alteration in the bodily symptoms rather than subjective awareness of anxiety.

This theory does explain some of the findings in the experiments described earlier. At the extreme of the somatic anxiety continuum are individuals who regard their bodily feelings as the sole cause of any subjective anxiety they experience. Their central nervous systems are so finely tuned to their bodily complaints that each missed heart beat, every nuance of the respiratory cycle and even the peristaltic movements of the bowel are signalled to the higher centres and force themselves into consciousness.

The author's theory is illustrated in FIGURE 21 and compared with the James–Lange hypothesis and the Richter–Breggin feedback hypothesis. Whereas the last relies on feedback on to pre-existing anxiety the author's hypothesis considers events before this 'expressed' anxiety is manifest. This does not deny the possibility of feed-back effects operating once anxiety has been experienced, so that the two views are not necessarily contradictory. The distinction between 'perceived' and 'expressed' anxiety is central to the original James–Lange hypothesis and in the author's theory these terms have been retained, although 'perceived' is given a rather different meaning, as relatively pure anxiety unaffected by bodily feelings. James used the term as a 'pre-emotional state', after appraisal of the emotional stimulus but before actual emotion was experienced. The emphasis on a dynamic equilibrium between psychic and bodily feelings in anxiety allows the presence of a

continuum between the extremes of each state. The resultant of this equilibrium is the 'expressed' or 'felt' anxiety, but as there is no way of defining emotional states apart from subjective expression, James' term is preferred.

There are clearly many factors which determine the emphasis an individual places on the many feelings experienced in anxiety. There is evidence that emphasis on bodily symptoms in affective disorders is affected by social class and intelligence (Rickels, Ward, and Schut, 1964) and cultural and

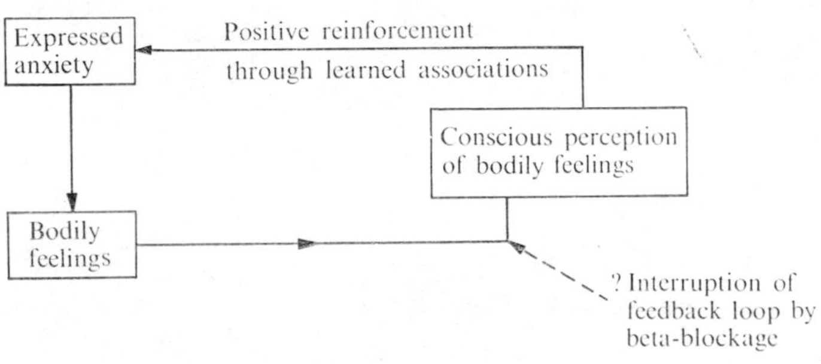

Richter–Breggin hypothesis

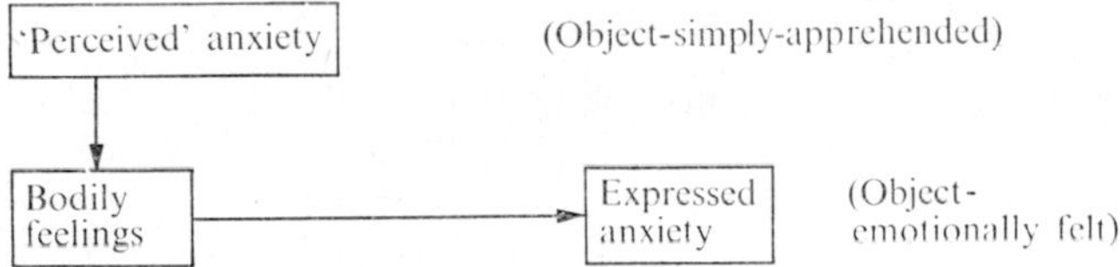

James–Lange hypothesis

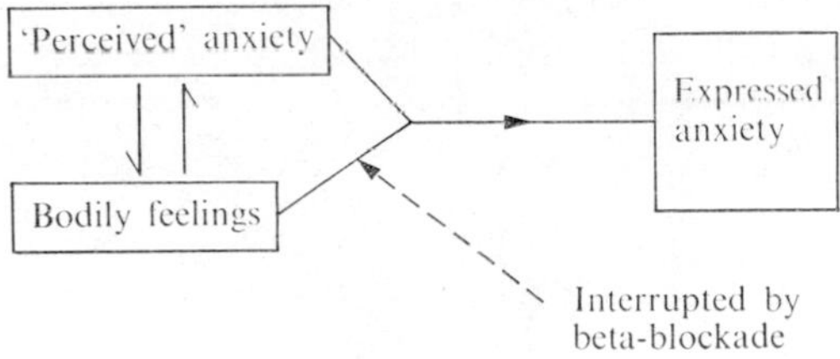

The author's hypothesis

Figure 21

ethnic origins (Allen German, 1972). These may be of primary importance but they could also be a secondary influence on whether or not a subject is aware of and recognizes an emotional stimulus. To take a simple example, the African tribesman with no knowledge of bodily function in anxiety, is more likely to regard an increase in heart rate under stress as a primary phenomenon than would a Western business executive who is constantly reminded of stress and its effects on the body.

This would not be of any importance if the resulting interpretations were not enduring ones. How long-lasting and to what extent they are influenced by direct intervention is not possible to answer. The somatically orientated

patient might gain insight through discussion of his symptoms with a doctor, or by psychotherapeutic intervention, and thus change his attitude towards his symptoms. There is evidence that such changes are more difficult to obtain than might at first sight appear (e.g. Misch, 1935). It is often considered a *sine qua non* of selection for psychotherapy that patients should be 'psychologically minded' and of above-average intelligence. Somatically anxious patients seldom satisfy these criteria and would not willingly submit themselves to psychological forms of treatment. Doctors in other medical specialties are very familiar with this group of patients who, even if not referred by general practitioners for further (organic) investigation of their symptoms, will find other ways of gaining hospital attention if their complaints persist. It is very unusual for this type of patient to be seen in a psychotherapy department, and even less common for any course of treatment to be completed satisfactorily. Continued denial of psychological causes of their symptoms usually brings summarily to an end any gentle exploration of the problem.

There is thus some evidence that somatic and psychic types are categorically sound. The implications of this are important if treatment produces differential responses in the two groups. In general medicine the distinction in symptomatology is seldom important except in understanding the many ways in which syndromes can present. Whether the patient with pernicious anaemia presents with lassitude, anorexia, or shortness of breath makes no difference to the type of treatment given.

In psychiatry symptoms are considered to be more important and diagnosis is based largely on syndromes—groups of symptoms occurring together. To many minds this illustrates the crudity of the subject as a medical discipline; Hunter (1973) castigates psychiatrists for failing to 'diagnose their patients like other doctors do', and allowing symptoms to be 'elevated to the status of disease like varieties of fever were in the eighteenth century'. This criticism would be apt if Hunter's claim that 'thorough investigation reveals a sufficient physical cause for the abnormal mental state in the majority of patients admitted to a district psychiatric hospital' were true. But it is not. Most patients presenting to a psychiatrist do not have organic disease and, in the absence of other sources of information, symptoms have acquired status in diagnosis and treatment. Originally this may have led to uncritical use and shallow thinking, but over the past seventy years the identification of discrete types of psychiatric disorder with different natural histories, genetic and environmental precipitants and mental states have confirmed that psychiatric symptoms are not tattered garments barely concealing the psychiatrist's scientific nudity, but respectable clothes that make up in function what they lack in finery.

The place of symptoms in psychiatry generally is relevant to the role of bodily symptoms in anxiety. The evidence of these studies suggests that the subject's interpretation of symptoms, as well as their nature, should be con-

patient might gain insight through discussion of his symptoms with a doctor, or by psychotherapeutic intervention, and thus change his attitude towards his symptoms. There is evidence that such changes are more difficult to obtain than might at first sight appear (e.g. Mayou, 1975). It is often considered a sine qua non of selection for psychotherapy that patients should be 'psychologically minded', and of above average intelligence. Somatically anxious patients seldom regard themselves as ill in this way and would not willingly submit themselves to psychological forms of treatment. Doctors in other medical specialities are familiar with this group of patients who, even if not referred by general practitioners [illegible]

sidered in diagnosis and management. Beta-adrenoceptor blocking drugs differ in their effects in somatic and psychic anxiety even when other clinical features are similar. The results indicate that propranolol may have a place in the treatment of a certain group of anxious patients. If the right patient is chosen, beta-blockade will be at least as effective as sedation with a centrally acting tranquillizer, and would therefore be preferred on the grounds of

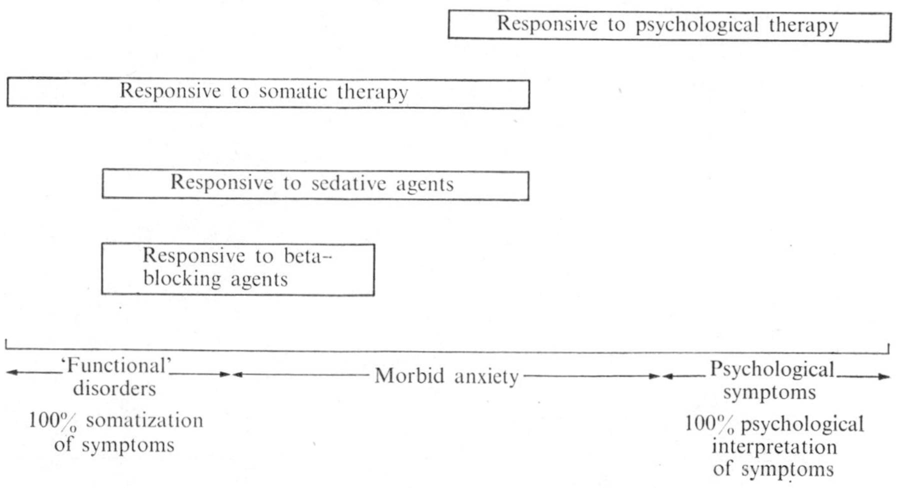

Figure 22

safety and absence of drug dependence. A somatic-psychic continuum might be constructed for morbid anxiety (and other affective states) illustrating the place of different types of treatment [FIG. 22].

The somatic extreme comes under the category of 'functional' disorders such as neurocirculatory asthenia, irritable colon, and effort syndrome. The cardiovascular disorders discussed in CHAPTER II are good examples of this group. At the other extreme are patients whose symptoms are almost entirely psychological with complaints of unbearable foreboding. The many treatments that are available for morbid anxiety are sketched in the diagram; they represent a consensus of current opinion and the boundaries are arbitrary. There is a division between the group that respond to psychological treatment in the broadest sense and that which responds to somatic therapies. The former consists of patients who look beyond immediate symptoms and hope to find the real cause for their unpleasant feelings. The latter group contains patients who limit their attention to immediate symptoms only and demand relief from these. They bridle at the suggestion that they are psychologically disturbed and much prefer to be investigated for organic disease than talk about their emotional feelings. To an external observer a patient from the first group has a correct appraisal of his condition, and the somatic complainer is apparently wrong in the interpretation of his symptoms. Yet he holds on to them against all evidence to the contrary. Why? The answer is that his own perceptions are correct and he cannot ignore them. When he becomes anxious

[illegible] ed in diagnosis and management. [illegible] differ in their effects in [illegible] and psychic anxiety [illegible] features are similar. The [illegible] indicate that [illegible] in the treatment of a certain group of anxious patients. If the [illegible] chosen, beta-blockade [illegible] at least as effective [illegible] sedation with a [illegible] acting tranquilliser, and [illegible] preferred on the [illegible]

[illegible] patients. The [illegible] group [illegible]

[illegible] symptoms only [illegible] relief from them [illegible] the suggestion that they [illegible] about their emotional [illegible]

In group [illegible] approach [illegible] is appropriate [illegible] there [illegible] his own perceptions [illegible] and he cannot [illegible] them. When he becomes anxious

the accompanying physiological changes are signalled to him loud and clear and are bound to be the prime object of his concern. Sedative drugs offer some relief to both groups because they act centrally, reducing both bodily symptomatology and psychological arousal, although even here there is evidence that patients who are more somatically orientated will respond more fully than those who seek a psychological explanation of their symptoms (Hesbacher *et al.*, 1970).

Whether or not the somatic–psychic division has general application is not pertinent to the subject of these investigations, but it illustrates that much of symptomatology can be considered in such terms. When bodily feelings are thought of in this way their importance in the genesis and maintenance of anxiety falls into perspective. If the psychic aspects of anxiety are predominant, the bodily manifestations become secondary features, fluctuating with differing levels of anxiety and perhaps causing concern at times of extreme emotion. In this situation, however, they never cause primary concern and may even reassure by their presence. It is worth noting that treatment with beta-blockade in such patients (and in normal subjects) produced marginally more anxiety than placebo [Chapters V and VIII] and it is possible that reduction in bodily feelings in those who are psychically anxious may be perceived as unpleasant. In the somatically anxious subject bodily feelings are paramount in perception and their direct alteration produces changes in mood. When Abraham Lincoln wrote 'I claim not to have controlled events, but confess plainly that events have controlled me', he could equally well have been describing the somatic-psychic dichotomy as the more lofty affairs of state. Man is sometimes a prisoner of his own bodily chains and his favourable response to their release is proof of this. It matters not that the interpretation of his feelings is a fiction; his perception of them is a fact, and he has to act on it. William James was mistaken when he made bodily feelings the conductor of the emotional orchestra, but for too long since they have played second fiddle. Their versatility should be recognized in emotional disorders when harmony has to be restored.

APPENDIX I

Characteristics of Patients in Somatic and Phychic Anxiety Groups

(CHAPTER VIII)

SOMATIC

1. Mr. P. L. (aged 32)—A patient with severe anxiety and hypochondriasis ever since adolescence. Had nocturnal enuresis in childhood, persisting until the age of 21. Admitted to hospital aged 23 for treatment of persistent anxiety and preoccupation about his physical health. He was convinced that he had cardiac disease and this was investigated on several occasions in hospital with negative results. His symptoms persisted after discharge and he continued to be concerned about his cardiac function. During attacks of palpitations he feared he would die, and this was his chief complaint on entry to the study. His inability to maintain social relationships and a steady occupation added to his symptoms.

Diagnosis: Chronic anxiety state with hypochondrical symptoms.

Response to treatment in trial: Responded to both propranolol and diazepam but expressed his main preference for the latter drug. Continued to take diazepam and propranolol (and later practolol) after finishing treatment in the trial. One year after finishing the trial he was still taking practolol alone as he found his symptoms returned if he stopped medication.

2. Mr. J. L. (aged 37)—A man with a two-year history of acute attacks of anxiety associated with headaches, tremor, abdominal discomfort, and paraesthesiae. On close questioning his symptoms seemed to be related to marital dissatisfaction but he maintained that his symptoms were the cause of his anxiety and did not relate these to his other problems. He had always been of an anxious predisposition but had never had attacks of panic before.

Diagnosis: Chronic anxiety state.

Response to treatment in trial: Made a definite preference for diazepam and a second choice for propranolol. Had a marked relapse when on placebo. Continued to take diazepam and six months later had been able to reduce this to the extent that he only needed it at a time of additional stress.

3. Mrs. V. S. (aged 23)—A sensitive married woman, with a 12-month history of anxiety and depression. This was felt to be associated with the difficulties in adjusting to her recent marriage. Had frequent attacks of fainting, trembling, and palpitations, associated with fears that she might become unconscious. Regarded these as the cause of her anxiety. She also had episodes when she felt depressed but had no other symptoms of depression apart from depressed mood.

Diagnosis: Anxiety state.

Response to treatment in trial: Responded equally well to all three drugs including placebo. Made no clear preferences for any one drug. Continued to be followed-up

in the next six months without much improvement, but her symptoms responded dramatically when she moved to a new house in a pleasant suburb. Six months later she was much improved on no medication.

4. Mrs. C. S. (aged 33)—An intelligent woman from a family in which five members had similar difficulties to those of the patient. Long-standing agoraphobic illness presenting when the patient was aged 20. Admitted to hospital at this time and responded well to desensitization. Remained fairly well over the next few years but her symptoms never entirely left her. Presented with fear of being alone because she had attacks of palpitations, headache, and severe weakness at these times. Regarded these as the cause of her anxiety and thought they might have a physical cause.

Diagnosis: Phobic anxiety state.

Response to treatment in trial: Made a first preference for propranolol and a second for diazepam. Continued on propranolol and occasional chlordiazepoxide after finishing treatment and symptoms improved significantly over the next six months and by then she had returned to work.

5. Mrs. A. B. (aged 21)—A young woman who first developed acute attacks of panic four months before assessment for the trial. Onset of attacks followed physical assault on the patient during which she received a head injury. Attacks of panic many times a day, preceded by flushing, dizziness, and palpitations. Although she related the onset of symptoms to her assault in temporal terms she maintained that they occurred as a consequence of her bodily symptoms.

Diagnosis: Anxiety state.

Response to treatment in trial: Made chief preference for diazepam and second for propranolol. Continued to take both drugs after completing trial, diazepam regularly and propranolol immediately after experiencing any physical symptoms. Was gradually able to reduce these. Six months later her symptoms were greatly improved.

6. Mr. B. P. (aged 23)—A young clerk with a three-year history of blushing in front of people which became so severe that he tried to avoid all company. Had also had attacks of palpitations, sweating, and trembling. Considered his blushing to be the cause of all his symptoms.

Diagnosis: Social phobia.

Response to treatment in trial: Made considerable improvement on both propranolol and diazepam but relapsed on placebo. Made equal preference for both active drugs and continued to take these. Steady improvement maintained during follow-up, his confidence increased and he widened his social contacts. Six months later was taking only 5 mgm chlordaizepoxide and 10 mgm propranolol daily and felt he no longer needed out-patient attendance.

PSYCHIC

1. Mr. C. H. (aged 52)—A postman who had long suffered from low self-esteem, anxiety, and phobic symptoms. First developed these when aged 27 and attended a psychiatrist at this time. Social fears became more intense in the year before assessment and he also developed a fear of heights.

Diagnosis: Complex phobic anxiety state.

at the next six months without much improvement, but [illegible] dramatically when she agreed to [illegible] she was much improved on maintenance.

4. Mrs. C. S. (aged 55).—An intelligent [illegible] whom the [illegible] had similar difficulties to those of the patient. Long-standing [illegible] illness presenting when the patient was [illegible]. Admitted to hospital for the first time and responded well to [illegible] but her symptoms never entirely [illegible] she had attacks of [illegible] Regarded [illegible] cause.

Diagnosis: [illegible]

Response [illegible]

5. Mrs. A. [illegible]

[illegible]

Diagnosis: [illegible]

Response [illegible]

[illegible]

1. Mr. C. H. (aged [illegible]).—[illegible] anxiety and [illegible] symptoms. First [illegible] psychiatrist [illegible] month [illegible]

Diagnosis: [illegible]

Response to treatment in trial: Made a clear preference for diaxepam and continued on this alone in small doses. Social anxieties improved during follow-up but height phobia persisted and was helped to some extent by behaviour therapy. Fifteen months after the trial he remained fairly well but was tending to depend on the hospital for continued support.

2. Mrs. R. D. (aged 40)—A housewife, unhappily married to an older man, who had been preoccupied with feelings of anxiety and loneliness for several years. At assessment was restless and tense but although highly anxious made no complaint of somatic symptoms, although she admitted these on questioning.

Diagnosis: Chronic anxiety state.

Response to treatment in trial: Made a clear preference for diazepam and a second choice for propranolol. Continued to take diazepam which only partially relieved her symptoms. Husband seen but no progress made in helping the marital relationship. Patient improved eventually after taking up yoga and performing voluntary work. One year after completing trial her improvement was still precarious.

3. Mr. E. W. (aged 39)—A lonely clerk with symptoms of tension and social anxieties for many years, worse since his twin brother was married and so saw less of the patient. Chief symptoms those of tension; had few somatic complaints. Was socially isolated and had low self-esteem.

Diagnosis: Anxiety state with social phobias.

Response to treatment in trial: Made a dramatic recovery on diazepam and was worse while on propranolol. Continued to take diazepam in low dosage. Was successful in obtaining another job and one year later was working happily in a holiday camp.

4. Mr. A. M. (aged 23)—A highly anxious young man who had been severely anxious for 2 years after experimenting with illicit drugs, particularly L.S.D. Frequent attacks of panic experienced, often with somatic symptoms, which were dismissed by the patient as of minor importance. Also had concern over his sexual orientation.

Diagnosis: Chronic anxiety state.

Response to treatment in trial: Clear preference for diazepam and second for placebo. Continued to take diazepam regularly during follow-up and symptomatically was much improved one year later. By this time he had reduced his diazepam but still needed to take it regularly.

5. Miss C. M. (aged 39)—A secretary who had experienced social anxiety and attacks of trembling for two years. These attacks occurred in company, particularly in the presence of eligible unmarried men. She blamed these attacks on her failure to find a suitable marriage partner. Had been generally anxious and irritable for many years.

Diagnosis: Chronic anxiety state with social phobias.

Response to treatment in trial: Responded to both placebo and diazepam, for which she expressed equal preference. Worse on propranolol, during which she noted respiratory difficulties. Continued on diazepam, but although this took the edge off her anxiety it did not lead to any improvement in her relationships. After nine months follow-up she was referred for behaviour therapy.

6. Mrs. F. B. (aged 36)—A severely agoraphobic woman with a five-year history of inability to travel outside the house alone. Had attacks of panic when outside, together with many somatic symptoms, but these symptoms were not thought to be important, and at no time was she concerned about her physical health.

Diagnosis: Agoraphobic syndrome.

Response to treatment in trial: Made a first choice for diazepam and second for placebo. Continued to take these after completing the trial and initially made very good progress. Was able to travel to shops alone for the first time in five years by taking diazepam immediately before going out. Improvement not maintained during follow-up and she was referred for behaviour therapy by 'flooding'. At six months follow-up she was making good progress.

6. **Miss F. F., (aged 46)** [illegible] of inability to travel outside [illegible] together with many phobic symptoms, [illegible] imprisoning, and at no time was she [illegible]

Diagnosis: Agoraphobic syndrome.

Response to treatment: [illegible] She continued to [illegible] good progress. [illegible] follow-up and she [illegible]

APPENDIX II

Characteristics of Patients in Somatic and Psychic Anxiety Groups

(CHAPTER IX)

SOMATIC

1. Mrs. E. M. (aged 62)—A chronically anxious woman who had suffered from feelings of panic and somatic symptoms for over fifteen years. Many years previously she had been widowed but in the past ten years had become dependent upon a man several years her junior. Uncertainty about the future of this relationship had accentuated her anxiety. She was admitted to hospital because this had become intolerable and she was convinced that she was going to die because her heart was going so fast. She complained frequently of palpitations and chest pain and was afraid to move in case attacks of panic and palpitations were precipitated.

Diagnosis: Chronic anxiety state with functional cardiovascular symptoms.

2. Mrs. Z. A. (aged 56)—An out patient with an eight year history of palpitations, pain down the left sternal margin, and difficulty in breathing. She had been investigated in hospital several times but no organic disease had been found. She was reluctant to attend a psychiatrist but only did so in the hope that a recommendation might be made for rehousing on medical grounds. She denied symptoms of anxiety or any other psychiatric symptoms at interview and asked frequently for tests of her cardiovascular function.

Diagnosis: Functional cardiovascular disorder.

3. Mr. T. W. (aged 21)—A young man with a fifteen month history of weight loss, nausea, and intermittent abdominal pain. Was referred from a gastroenterology clinic after investigation had shown no organic basis for his symptoms. Symptoms occurred mainly before social occasions and appeared to be increased when he thought about his forthcoming marriage. Denied anxiety or other psychiatric symptoms at interview.

Diagnosis: Functional gastro-intestinal disorder.

4. Mrs. B. R. (aged 20)—A young woman with a three year history of nausea and vomiting without apparent cause. Was referred from a gastroenterology clinic after no physical basis was found for her symptoms. At interview she admitted getting anxious in social situations and had noted that her symptoms had occurred when eating in public. These had then generalized so that her somatic symptoms occurred at any meal which she was eating in company.

Diagnosis: Functional gastro-intestinal disorder.

5. Miss S. E. (aged 17)—A young girl with a two year history of excessive flatulence for which no organic cause had been found. Symptoms occurred soon after moving

house. The patient strongly denied any psychological symptoms and only came with great reluctance to see a psychiatrist.

Diagnosis: Functional gastro-intestinal disorder.

6. Mrs. I. B. (aged 26)—A young married woman who had been chronically anxious ever since adolescence. In addition to free-floating anxiety also had multiple phobias, including claustrophobia, fear of the dark, fear of spiders, and balloons. Presented with these symptoms and a three-year history of nausea and stomach pains, occurring when she was outside her home, particularly when she was with other people. Physical investigations had failed to reveal any abnormality and when seen she was prepared to admit that these symptoms could be related to her long-standing anxiety.

Diagnosis: Chronic anxiety state with phobic symptoms.

PSYCHIC

1. Mrs. N. J. (aged 50)—A woman with a twenty-year history of attacks of anxiety and inability to cope under stress. Had received treatment in hospital on five previous occasions without lasting benefit. Anxiety was free-floating and was often exacerbated without apparent cause. Also had additional symptoms, including trembling and epigastric discomfort but regarded these as secondary to her anxieties. Was an in-patient when she took part in the study.

Diagnosis: Chronic anxiety state.

2. Mrs. S. C. (aged 20)—A young lady who had always been anxiety prone but had become much more anxious in the year before assessment. She also developed phobic symptoms and was afraid of being alone in her house, particularly in the dark. Her husband was not able to understand her symptoms and this had led to a deterioration in their marital relationship. When seen as an outpatient she was anxious and also had noted some palpitations but was not concerned about these.

Diagnosis: Phobic anxiety state in an anxiety prone personality.

3. Mr. A. K. (aged 33)—A computer engineer who had become excessively anxious in the year before assessment. He had always been anxiety prone and highly conscientious. Extra responsibility at work appeared to be the immediate cause of his anxiety. He had frequent attacks of panic for no reason and although he experienced some somatic symptoms, particularly stomach pains, he related these to his anxious symptoms.

Diagnosis: Anxiety state.

4. Mr. K. D. (aged 30)—An engineer who had become dissatisfied with his profession and had become increasingly frustrated, anxious, and irritable. Because of his dissatisfaction he had decided to give up his job and study to be a dentist. This entailed financial sacrifice and long hours of study. When seen the additional stress of this work had increased his anxiety and he was unable to concentrate. He was convinced that his symptoms were a direct consequence of his long hours of study and financial stresses.

He complained of no somatic symptoms.

Diagnosis: Anxiety state.

REFERENCES

ADLER, A. (1917) *The neurotic constitution*, Translated by B. Glueck and J. E. Lind, New York.

AHLQUIST, R. P. (1948) A study of the adrenotropic receptors, *Am. J. Physiol.*, **153**, 586–99.

AHLQUIST, R. P. (1967) Development of the concept of alpha and beta adrenotropic receptors, *Ann. N.Y. Acad. Sci.*, **139**, 549–52.

AITKEN, R. C. B. (1969) Measurement of feelings using visual analogue scales, *Proc. r. Soc. Med.*, **62**, 989–93.

AITKEN, R. C. B. and ZEALLEY, A. K. (1970) Measurement of moods, *Br. J. hosp. Med.* **4**, 215–24.

ALLEN, J. A., ARMSTRONG, J. E., and RODDIE, I. C. (1973) The regional distribution of emotional sweating in man, *J. Physiol.*, **235**, 749–59.

ALLEN GERMAN, G. (1972) Aspects of clinical psychiatry in Sub-Saharan Africa, *Br. J. Psychiatry*, **121**, 461–79.

ALTSCHULE, M. D. (1953) *Bodily physiology in mental and emotional disorders*, New York.

ARBAB, A. G., BONN, J. A., and HICKS, D. C. (1971) Effect of propranolol on lactate induced phenomena in normal subjects, *Br. J. Pharmacol.*, **41**, 430P.

ARIËNS, E. J. (1967) The structure-activity relationships of beta-adrenergic drugs and beta-adrenergic blocking drugs, *Ann. N.Y. Acad. Sci.*, **139**, 606–32.

ARIËNS, E. J., VAN ROSSUM, J. M., and SIMONIS, A. M. (1957) Affinity, intrinsic activity and drug interactions, *Pharmacol. Rev.*, **9**, 218–36.

ARISTOTLE. (1912) *The Works of Aristotle*, English Translation, edited by Smith, J. A. and Ross, W. D., Oxford.

ARMITAGE, P. (1960) *Sequential medical trials*; Oxford.

ARNOLD, M. B. (1950) An excitatory theory of emotion, in *Feelings and Emotions: the Mooseheart symposium*, pp. 11–33, New York.

ATSMON, A., BLUM, I., WIJSENBEEK, H., MAOZ, B., STEINER, M., and ZIEGELMAN, G. (1971) The short-term effects of adrenergic-blocking agents in a small group of psychotic patients, *Psychiat., Neurol., Neurochir.*, **74**, 251–8.

AX, A. F. (1953) The physiological differentiation between fear and anger in humans, *Psychosom. Med.*, **15**, 433–42.

AXELROD, J. (1965) The metabolism, storage and release of catecholamines, *Recent Prog. horm. Res.*, **21**, 597–619.

BAINBRIDGE, J. G. and GREENWOOD, D. T. (1971) Tranquillising effects of propranolol demonstrated in rats, *Neuropharmacology*, **10**, 453–8.

BARD, P. (1928) A diencephalic mechanism for the expression of rage with special reference to the sympathetic nervous system, *Am. J. Physiol.*, **84**, 490–515.

BARNETT, A. (1938) The phase angle of normal human skin, *J. Physiol.*, **93**, 349–66.

BARRETT, A. M. and CULLUM, V. A. (1968) The biological properties of the optical isomers of propranolol and their effects on cardiac arrhythmias, *Br. J. Pharmacol.*, **34**, 43–55.

BASOWITZ, H., KORCHIN, S. J., OKEN, D., GOLDSTEIN, M. S., and GUSSACK, H. (1956) Anxiety and performance changes with minimal doses of epinephrine, *Arch. Neurol. Psychiatry*, **76**, 98–106.

BEKES, M., MATOS, L., RAUSCH, J., and TÖRÖK, E. (1968) Treatment of migraine with propranolol, *Lancet*, **ii**, 980.

BELLEAU, P. (1967) Stereochemistry of adrenergic receptors: newer concepts on the molecular mechanism of action of catecholamines and antiadrenergic drugs at the receptor level, *Ann. N.Y. Acad. Sci.*, **139**, 580–606.

BERGAMASCO, B. (1967) Modifications of cortical responsiveness in humans induced by drugs acting on the central nervous system, *Electroencephalogr., clin. Neurophysiol.*, **23**, 191.

BERRY, C., GELDER, M. G., and SUMMERFIELD (1965) The experimental analysis of drug effects on human performance using information theory concepts, *Br. J. Psychol.*, **56**, 255–65.

BESTERMAN, E. M. M. and FRIEDLANDER, D. H. (1965) Clinical experiences with propranolol, *Postgrad. med. J.*, **41**, 526–35.

BINDRA, D. (1969) A unified interpretation of emotion and motivation, *Ann. N.Y. Acad. Sci.*, **159**, 1071–83.

BLACK, J. W., DUNCAN, W. A. M. and SHANKS, R. G. (1965) Comparison of some properties of pronethalol and propranolol, *Br. J. Pharmacol.*, **25**, 577–91.

BLACKMAN, R. B. and TURKEY, J. W. (1959) *The measurement of power spectra*, New York.

BLAKE, M. J. F. (1967) Time of day effects on performance in a range of tasks, *Psychonomic Sci.*, **9**, 349–50.

BOGDONOFF, M. D., HARLAN, W. R., ESTES, Jr. E. H., and KIRSHNER, N. (1959) Changes in urinary catecholamines excretion accompanying carbohydrate and lipid responses to oral examination, *Circulation*, **20**, 674.

BOLLINGER, A., GANDER, M., PYLKKÄNEN, P. O., and FORSTER, G. (1966) Treatment of the hyperkinetic heart syndrome with propranolol, *Cardiologia* (Basel) Supplement 2, **49**, 68–82.

BOND, P. A. (1967) Metabolism of propranolol ('Inderal'), a potent, specific beta-adrenergic receptor blocking agent, *Nature*, **213**, 721.

BOND, A. J. (1972) Unpublished Ph.D. thesis, University of London.

BOND, A. J. and LADER, M. H. (1972) Residual effects of hypnotics, *Psychopharmacologia*, **25**, 117–32.

BOND, A. J. and LADER, M. H. (1973) Residual effects of flurazepam, *Psychopharmacologia*, **32**, 223–35.

BOND, A. J. and LADER, M. H. (1974) The use of analog scales in rating subjective feelings, *Br. J. med. Psychol.* (in press).

BONN, J. A. and TURNER, P. (1971) D-propranolol and anxiety, *Lancet*, **i**, 1355–6.

BONN, J. A., TURNER, P., and HICKS, D. C. (1972) Beta-adrenergic-receptor blockade with practolol in treatment of anxiety, *Lancet*, **i**, 814–15.

BRAZIER, M. A. B., FINESINGER, J. E., and COBB, S. (1945) A contrast between the electroencephalograms of 100 psychoneurotic adults and those of 500 normal adults, *Am. J. Psychiatry*, **101**, 443–8.

BREGGIN, P. R. (1964) The psychophysiology of anxiety: with a review of the literature concerning adrenaline, *J. ner. ment. Dis.*, **139**, 558–68.

BREWER, C. (1972) Beneficial effect of beta-adrenergic blocking agents on 'exam. nerves', *Lancet*, **ii**, 435.

BROWN, C. C. (1967) Editor, *Methods in Psychophysiology*, Baltimore.

BROWN, J. S. and FARBER, I. E. (1951) Emotions conceptualized as intervening variables—with suggestions toward a theory of frustration, *Psychol. Bull.*, **48**, 465–95.

BRYAN, P. C., EFIONG, D. O., STEWART-JONES, J., and TURNER P. (1974) Propranolol

on tests of visual acuity and central nervous activity, *Br. J. clin. Phrmacol.*, **1**, 82–4.

CALDWELL, D. F. and CROMWELL, R. L. (1959) Replication report: The relationship of manifest anxiety and electric shock to eyelid conditioning, *J. exp. Psychol.*, **57**, 348–9.

CANNON, W. B. (1927) The James–Lange theory of emotions: a critical examination and an alternative theory, *Am. J. Psychol.*, **39**, 106–24.

CANNON, W. B. (1929) *Bodily changes in pain, hunger, fear and rage*, New York. 2nd edition.

CANNON, W. B. (1931) Again the James–Lange and the thalamic theories of emotion, *Psychol. Rev.*, **38**, 281–95.

CANNON, W. B. and ROSENLUETH, A. (1937) *Autonomic neuro-effector systems*, New York.

CANTRIL, H. and HUNT, W. A. (1932) Emotional effects produced by injection of adrenaline, *Am. J. Psychol.*, **44**, 300–7.

CARLSSON, C. and HAGGENDAL, J. (1967) Arterial noradrenaline levels after ethanol withdrawal, *Lancet*, **ii**, 889.

CARLSSON, C. and JOHANSSON, T. (1971) The psychological effects of propranolol in the abstinence phase of chronic alcoholics, *Br. J. Psychiatry*, **119**, 605–6.

CHARCOT, J. M. (1889) *Clinical lectures on diseases of the nervous system.* 1st edition, **3**, 183–97. Translated by T. Savill. London.

CHAI, C. Y. and WANG, S. C. (1966) Cardiovascular actions of diazepam in the cat, *J. Pharmacol. exp. Ther.*, **154**, 271–80.

CLARK, A. J. (1933) *Mode of action of drugs on cells*, London.

CLEGHORN, J. M., PETERFRY, G., PINTER, E. J., and PATTEE, C. J. (1970) Verbal anxiety and the beta-adrenergic receptors: a facilitating mechanism? *J. nerv. ment. Dis.*, **151**, 266–72.

COLQUOHOUN, W. P. (1969) Editor, *Aspects of human efficiency: diurnal rhythm and loss of sleep*, London.

COLTART, D. J. and SHAND, D. G. (1970) Plasma propranolol levels in the quantitative assessment of beta-adrenergic blockade in man, *Br. med. J.*, **3**, 731–4.

COLTART, D. J., GIBSON, D. G., and SHAND, D. G. (1971) Plasma propranolol levels associated with suppression of ventricular ectopic beats, *Br. med. J.*, **1**, 490–1.

CONWAY, M. (1971) Final examinations, *Practitioner*, **206**, 795–800.

COPPEN, A. J. and MEZEY, A. G. (1960) The influence of sodium amytal on the respiratory anbormalities of anxious psychiatric patients, *J. psychosom. Res.*, **5**, 52–5.

CRISP, A. H. (1966) 'Transference', 'symptom emergence' and 'social repercussion' in behaviour therapy, *Br. J. med. Psychol.*, **39**, 179–96.

CROMWELL, H. A. (1963) Controlled evaluation of psychotherapeutic drug in internal medicine, *Clin. Med.*, **70**, 2239–44.

CURTIS, F. R. (1929) The sympathomimetic action of ephedrine, *J. Pharmacol. exp. Ther.*, **35**, 333–41.

DALE, H. H. (1906) On some physiological actions of ergot, *J. Physiol.*, **34**, 163–206.

DALE, H. H. and FELDBERG, W. (1934) The chemical transmission of secretory impulses to the sweat glands of the cat, *J. Physiol.*, **82**, 121–8.

DANA, C. L. (1921) The anatomic seat of the emotions: a discussion of the James–Lange theory, *Arch. Neurol. Psychiatry*, **6**, 634–40.

DARROW, C. W. (1934) The significance of the galvanic skin reflex in the light of its relation to quantitative measurements of perspiration, *Psychol. Bull.*, **31**, 697–8.

DARWIN, C. (1872) *The expression of emotion in man and animals*, London.

DAWSON, G. D. (1951) A summation technique for detecting small signals in a large irregular background, *J. Physiol.*, **115**, 2P-3P.

DESCARTES, R. (1648) *Passions de l'âme*, Paris. English translation—The Philosophical works of Descartes, volume 1. Translated by E. S. Haldane and G. R. T. Ross, 1911, Cambridge.

DICKENS, D. W., LADER, M. H., and STEINBERG, H. (1965) Differential effects of two amphetamine-barbiturate mixtures in man, *Br. J. Pharmacol.*, **24**, 14–23.

DOLLERY, C. T., PATERSON, J. W., and CONOLLY, M. E. (1969) Clinical pharmacology of beta-receptor-blocking drugs, *Clin. Pharmacol. Ther.*, **10**, 765–99.

DOMINO, E. F. (1967) Effects of pre-anaesthetic drugs on visually evoked responses, *Anaesthesiology*, **28**, 184–91.

DORNHORST, A. C. and ROBINSON, B. F. (1962) Clinical pharmacology of a beta-adrenergic blocking agent (nethalide), *Lancet*, **ii**, 314–16.

DUFFY, E. (1962) *Activation and behaviour*, New York.

DUFFY, E. and LACEY, O. L. (1946) Adaptation in energy mobilisation: changes in general skin conductance, *J. exp. Psychol.*, **36**, 437–52.

DUNLEAVY, D. L. F., MACLEAN, A. W., and OSWALD, I. (1971) Debrisoquine, guanethidine, propranolol and human sleep, *Psychopharmacologia*, **21**, 101–10.

DYNES, J. B. and TOD, H. (1940) Emotional and somatic responses of schizophrenic patients and normal controls to adrenaline and doryl, *J. Neurol. Psychiatry*, **3**, 1–8.

EDMONSON, H. D., ROSCOE, B., and VICKERS, M. D. (1972) Biochemical evidence of anxiety in dental patients, *Br. med. J.*, **4**, 7–9.

EDWARDS, A. L. (1965) *Experimental design in psychological research*, revised edition, New York.

ELIASCH, H., LAGER, C. G., NORBÄCK, K., ROSEN, A., and SCOTT, H. (1967) The beta-adrenergic receptor blockade modification of the systemic haemodynamic effects of link trainer simulated flight. In 'Emotional stress, physiological and psychological reactions: Medical, industrial and military implications'. *Försvarmedicin*, **3**, supp. 2, 120–9, Stockholm.

ELLINGSON, R. J. (1954) The incidence of E.E.G. abnormality among patients with mental disorders of apparently non-organic origin: a critical review, *Am. J. Psychiatry*, **11**, 263–75.

ELMADJIAN, F. E., HOPE, J. M., and LAMSON, B. A. (1957) Excretion of epinephrine and norepinephrine in various emotional states, *J. clin. Endocrinol.*, **17**, 608–20.

EULER, U. S. VON (1946) A specific sympathomimetic ergone in adrenergic nerve fibres (sympathin) and its relations to adrenaline and noradrenaline, *Acta physiol. Scand.*, **12**, 73–97.

EULER, U. S. VON (1966) Release and uptake of noradrenaline in adrenergic nerve granules, *Acta physiol. scand.*, **67**, 430–40.

EULER, U. S. VON and HELLNER, S. (1952) Noradrenaline excretion in muscular work, *Acta physiol scand.*, **26**, 183–91.

EULER, U. S. VON and LUNDBERG, J. (1954) Effect of flying on the epinephrine excretion in air force personnel, *J. appl. Physiol.*, **6**, 551–5.

FEINSTEIN, A. R. (1973) Ambiguity and abuse in the twelve different concepts of 'Control', *Clin. Pharmacol. Ther.*, **14**, 112–22.

FENZ, W. D. and EPSTEIN, S. (1967) Gradients of physiological arousal of experimental and novice parachutists as a function of an approaching jump, *Psychosom. Med.*, **29**, 33–51.

FINK, M. (1969) E.E.G. and human psychopharmacology, *Ann. Rev. Pharmacol.*, **9**, 241–58.

FINKLEMAN, B. (1930) On the nature of inhibition in the intestine, *J. Physiol.*, **70**, 145–57.

FITZGERALD, J. D. (1969) Perspectives in adrenergic beta receptor blockade, *Clin. Pharmacol. Ther.*, **10**, 292–306.

FITZGERALD, J. D. (1971) In 'Advances in adrenergic beta-receptor therapy'. Post-graduate *med. J.*, suppl. **47**, 38.

FITZGERALD, J. D. and SCALES, B. (1968) Effect of a new adrenergic beta-blocking agent (ICI 50172) on heart rate in relation to its blood levels, *Int. J. clin. Pharmacol.*, **1**, 467–74.

FOULDS, G. (1965) *Personality and Personal Illness*, London.

FRANKENHAUSER, M., JÄRPE, G., and MATELL, G. (1961) Effects of intravenous infusions of adrenaline and noradrenaline on certain psychological and physiological functions, *Acta physiol. scand.*, **51**, 175–86.

FREEMAN, G. L. (1948) *Physiological psychology*, New York.

FREUD, S. (1894) The justification for detaching from neurasthenia a particular syndrome: the anxiety-neurosis. In *Collected Papers*, (1924) **1**, 76–106, London.

FREUD, S. (1949) *An outline of psychoanalysis*, London.

FRITH, C. D. (1967) The effect of nicotine on tapping, *Life Sci.*, **6**, 313–19.

FROHLICH, E. D., DUNSTAN, H. P., and PAGE, I. H. (1966) Hyperdynamic beta-adrenergic circulatory state, *Arch. int. Med.*, **117**, 614–19.

FUNKENSTEIN, D. H. (1955) The physiology of fear and anger, *Sci. Am.*, **192**, 74–80.

FUXE, K., DAHLSTRÖM, A., and HILLARP, N. A. (1965) Central monoamine neurones and monoamine neuro-transmission, *Proc. 23rd int. Physiol. Congr.*, **4**, 419–31.

GADDUM, J. H. (1926) The action of adrenaline and ergotamine on the uterus of the rabbit, *J. Physiol.*, **61**, 141–50.

GAULT, J. E. (1966) The treatment of nervous palpitations, *Med. J. Aust.*, **1**, 37.

GEORGE, C. F., FENYVESI, T., CONOLLY, M. E., and DOLLERY, C. T. (1972) Pharmacokinetics of dextro-, laevo- and racemic propranolol in man, *Eur. J. clin. Pharmacol.*, **4**, 74–6.

GILLAM, P. M. S. and PRICHARD, B. N. C. (1965) Use of propranolol in angina pectoris, *Br. med. J.*, **2**, 337–9.

GILLIGAN, B. S., VEALE, J. L., and WODAK, J. (1972) Propranolol in the treatment of tremor, *Med. J. Aust.*, **1**, 320–2.

GOMOLL, A. W. (1970) Beta-adrenergic blocking drugs, propranolol and sotalol: effects of myocardial contractility and hemodynamics, *Fed. Proc.*, **29**, 476.

GORLIN, R. (1962) The hyperkinetic heart syndrome, *J. Am., med. Assoc.*, **182**, 823–9.

GOTTSCHALK, L. A., STONE, W. N., and GLESER, G. C. (1974) Peripheral versus central mechanism(s) accounting for anti-anxiety effect of propranolol, *Psychosom. Med.*, **36**, 47–56.

GRAHAM, J. D. P. (1945) Static tremor in anxiety states, *J. Neurol., Neurosur. Psychiatry*, **8**, 57–60.

GRANVILLE-GROSSMAN, K. L. and TURNER, P. (1966) The effect of propranolol on anxiety, *Lancet*, **i**, 788–90.

GROSZ, H. J. (1972) Narcotic withdrawal symptoms in heroin users treated with propranolol, *Lancet*, **ii**, 564–6.

HADDEN, D. R., MONTGOMERY, D. A., SHANKS, R. G., and WEAVER, J. A. (1968) Propranolol and iodine—131 in the management of thyrotoxicosis, *Lencet*, **2**, 852–4.

HAMILTON, M. (1959) The assessment of anxiety states by rating, *Br. J. med. Psychol.*, **32**, 50–5.

HAMILTON, M. (1969) Diagnosis and rating of anxiety, In *Studies of Anxiety*, ed. M. H. Lader, *Br. J. Psychiatry*, Special Publ. No. 3, pp. 76–9.

HAMMOND, P. H., MERTON, P. A., and SUTTON, G. G. (1956) Nervous gradation of muscular contraction, *Br. med. Bull.*, **12**, 214–18.

HARRIS, W. S. (1965) On the mechanisms causing hyperkinetic circulation in chronic anxiety states, *J. lab. clin. Med.*, **66**, 875–6.

HARRIS, W. S., SCHOENFELD, C. D., GWYNNE, P. H., WEISSLER, A. M., and WARREN, J. V. (1964) Circulatory and humoral responses to fear and anger, *J. lab. clin. Med.*, **64**, 867.

HARRISON, D. C. (1972) Beta adrenergic blockade, 1972. Pharmacology and clinical uses, *Am. J. Cardiol.*, **29**, 432–5.

HATHAWAY, S. R. and MEEHL, P. E. (1951) *An atlas for the clinical use of the M.M.P.I.* Minneapolis.

HEBB, D. O. (1946a) Emotion in man and animal: an analysis of the intuitive processes of recognition, *Psychol. Rev.*, **53**, 88–100.

HEBB, D. O. (1946b) On the nature of fear, *Psychol. Rev.*, **53**, 259–76.

HEPPENSTALL, M. E., HILL, D., and SLATER, E. (1945) The E.E.G. in the prognosis of war neurosis, *Brain*, **68**, 17–22.

HERRING, A. B. (1964) Action of pronethalol on Parkinsonian tremor, *Lancet*, **ii**, 892.

HESBACHER, P. T., RICKELS, K., HUTCHINSON, J., RAAB, E., SABLASKY, L., WHALEN, E. M., and PHILLIPS, F. J. (1970) Setting, patients and doctor effects on drug response in neurotic patients: II Differential improvement, *Psychopharmacologia*, **18**, 209–226.

HILGARD, E. R. (1956) *Theories of learning* (2nd edition), New York.

HILL, D. (1963) The E.E.G. in psychiatry, in *Electroencephalography*, 2nd. edition, ed. J. D. N. Hill and G. Parr, 368–428, London.

HILLARP, N. A., FUXE, K., and DAHLSTRÖM, A. (1966) Demonstration and mapping of central neurons containing dopamine, noradrenaline and 5-hydroxytryptamine and their reactions to psychopharmaca, *Pharmacol. Rev.*, **18**, 727–41.

HINSHELWOOD, R. D. (1969) Hallucinations and propranolol, *Br. med. J.*, **2**, 445.

HOLMBERG, G., LEVI, L., MATHE, A., ROSEN, A., and SCOTT, H. (1967) Plasma catecholamines and the effects of adrenergic beta-receptor blockade on cardiovascular reactions and subjective feelings during emotional stress. In *Emotional stress, physiological and psychological reactions: Medical, industrial and military implications*, *Försvarmedicin*, **3**, supp. 2, 201–21, Stockholm.

HOLMGREN, A., JONSSON, B., LEVANDER, L., LINDERHOLM, A., SJÖSTRAND, T., and STRÖM, G. (1957) Low physical working in suspected heart cases due to inadequate adjustment of peripheral blood flow (vasoregulatory asthenia), *Acta med. scand.*, **158**, 437–46.

HOWE, E. S. (1958) G.S.R. conditioning in anxiety states, normals and chronic functional schizophrenic subjects, *J. abnorm. soc. Psychol.*, **56**, 183–9.

HOWE, R. and SHANKS, R. G. (1966) Optical isomers of propranolol, *Nature*, **210**, 1336–8.

HOWITT, G. and ROWLANDS, D. J. (1966) Beta-sympathetic blockade in hyperthyroidism, *Lancet*, **1**, 628–31.

HUNNINGHAKE, D. B., AZARNOFF, D. L., and WAXMAN, D. (1967) Drug inhibition of catecholamine-induced metabolic effects in humans, *Ann. N.Y. Acad. Sci.*, **139**, 971–81.

HUNTER, R. (1973) Psychiatry and neurology: psychosyndrome or brain disease, *Proc. roy. Soc. Med.*, **66**, 359–64.

JAMES, W. (1884) What is an emotion? *Mind*, **9**, 188–205.

JAMES, W. (1891) *Principles of Psychology*, **2**, 442–85, London.

JASPER, H. H. (1958) The ten twenty electrode system of the International Federation, *Electroencephalogr. clin. Neirophysiol.*, **10**, 371–5.

JARVIS, M. J., and LADER, M. H. (1971) The effects of nitrous oxide on the auditory evoked response in a reaction time task. *Psychopharmacologia* **20**, 201–12.

JENNER, F. A. and KERRY, R. J. (1967) Comparison of diazepam, chlordiazepoxide and amylobarbitone. A multidose double-blind crossover study, *Dis. nerv. Sys.*, **28**, 245–9.

JOYCE, C. R. B. (1968) Psychological factors in the controlled evaluation of therapy, in *Psychopharmacology, Dimensions and Perspectives*. ed. C. R. B. Joyce, 215–42.

KELLNER, R. (1972) Improvement criteria in drug trials with neurotic patients, *Psychol. Med.*, **2**, 73–80.

KELLY, D. H. W. (1966) Measurement of anxiety by forearm blood flow, *Br. J. Psychiatry*, **112**, 789–98.

KORNETSKY, C., VATES, T. S., and KESSLER, E. K. (1959) A comparison of hypnotic and residual psychological effects of chloropromazine and secobarbital in man, *J. Pharmacol. exp. Ther.*, **127**, 51–4.

KREITMAN, N. (1961) The reliability of psychiatric diagnosis, *J. ment. Sci.*, **107**, 876–86.

KUNO, Y. (1956) *The physiology of human perspiration*, Oxford.

LACEY, J. I. (1967) Somatic response patterning and stress: some revisions of activation theory, in *Psychological Stress: Issues in research*, ed. M. H. Appley and R. Trumbull, New York.

LACEY, J. I. and VANLEHN, R. (1952) Differential response in somatic response to stress, *Psychosom. Med.*, **14**, 71–81.

LACEY, J. I., BATEMAN, D. E., and VANLEHN, R. (1953) Autonomic response specificity, an experimental study, *Psychosom. Med.*, **15**, 8–21.

LACEY, J. I. and LACEY, B. C. (1958a) Verification and extension of the principle of autonomic response stereotypy, *Am. J. Psychol.*, **71**, 50–73.

LACEY, J. I. and LACEY, B. C. (1958b) In *Brain and Human Behaviour*, ed. Williams and Wilkins, Baltimore.

LACEY, O. L. (1950) Individual differences in somatic response pattern, *J. comp. physiol. Psychol.*, **43**, 338–50.

LACEY, O. L. and SEIGEL, P. S. (1949) An analysis of the unit of measurement of the galvanic skin response, *J. exp. Psychol.*, **39**, 122–7.

LADER, M. H. (1963) Unpublished Ph.D. Thesis.

LADER, M. H. (1969) Psychophysiology of anxiety, in *Studies of Anxiety*, ed. M. H. Lader, *Br. J. Psychiatry*, Special Publication, No. 3, 53–61.

LADER, M. H. and MARKS, I. M. (1971) *Clinical anxiety*, London.

LADER, M. H. and MONTAGU, J. D. (1962) The psycho-galvanic reflex; a pharmacological study of the peripheral mechanism, *J. Neurol. Neurosurg. Psychiatry*, **25**, 126–33

LADER, M. H. and NORRIS, H. (1969) The effects of nitrous oxide on the auditory evoked response, *Psychopharmacologia*, **16**, 115–27

LADER, M. H. and TYRER, P. J. (1972) Central and peripheral effects of propranolol and sotalol in normal human subjects, *Br. J. Pharmacol.* **45**, 557–60.

LADER, M. H. and WING, L. (1966) *Physiological measures, sedative drugs and morbid anxiety*, London.

LANGE, C. G. (1885) *Om Sindsbevägelser*, Copenhagen. (German translation: *Ueber Gemüthsbewegungen*, by H. Kurella, 1887, Leipzig.) (English translation: *The Emotions*, 33–90. Edited by K. Dunlap, 1921, New York.)

LANGLEY, J. N. (1905) On the reactions of cells and of nerve-endings to certain

poisons, chiefly as regards the reaction of striated muscle to nicotine and curari, *J. Physiol.*, **33**, 374–413.

LEEPER, R. W. (1948) A motivational theory of emotion to replace 'emotion as disorganised response', *Psychol. Rev.*, **55**, 5–21.

LESZKOVSKY, G. and TARDOS, L. (1965) Some effects of propranolol on the central nervous system. *J. Pharm. Pharmacol.*, **17**, 518–19.

LEVI, L. (1965) The urinary output of adrenalin and noradrenaline during pleasant and unpleasant emotional states. A preliminary report, *Psychosom. Med.*, **27**, 80–85.

LINDEMANN, E. and FINESINGER, J. E. (1938) The effect of adrenalin and mecholyl in states of anxiety in psychoneurotic patients, *Am. J. Psychiatry*, **95**, 353–70.

LINDSLEY, D. B. (1951) Emotion, in *Handbook of Experimental Psychology*, ed. S. S. Stevens, New York.

LINDSLEY, D. B. (1952) Psychological phenomena and the electroencephalogram, *Electroencephalogr. clin. Neurophysiol.*, **4**, 443–56.

LINDSLEY, D. B., BOWDEN, J. W., and MAGOUN, H. W. (1949) Effect upon the electroencephalogram of acute injury to the brain stem activating system, *J. Electroencephalogr. clin. Neurophysiol.*, **1**, 475–86.

LINDSLEY, D. B., SCHREINER, L. H., KNOWLES, W. D., and MAGOUN, H. W. (1950) Behavioural and electroencephalographic changes following chronic brain-stem lesions in the cat, *J. Electroencephalogr. clin. Neurophysiol.*, **2**, 483–98.

LISH, P. M., SHELANSKI, M. V., LABUDDE, J. A., and WILLIAMS, W. R. (1967) Inhibition of cardiac chronotropic action of isoproterenol by sotalol (MJ 1999) in rat, dog and man, *Curr. ther. Res.*, **9**, 311–24.

LITTLE, J. C. and MCPHAIL, N. I. (1973) Measures of depressive mood at monthly intervals, *Br. J. Psychiatry*, **122**, 447–52.

LYKKEN, D. T. (1959) Properties of electrodes used in electrodermal measurements, *J. comp. physiol. Psychol.*, **52**, 629–34.

MACDONALD, A. G., INGRAM, C. G., and MCNEILL, R. S. (1967) The effect of propranolol on airway resistance, *Br. J. Anaesth.*, **39**, 919–26.

MACLEAN, P. D. (1955) The limbic system (visceral brain) and emotional behaviour, *Arch. Neurol. Psychiatry*, **73**, 130–4.

MALEBRANCHE, N. (1674) *Recherche de la vérité*, **2**, 147–60, Paris.

MALMO, R. B. (1959) Activation: a neuropsychological dimension, *Psychol. Rev.*, **66**, 367–86.

MALMO, R. B., SHAGASS, C., DAVIS, J. F., CLEGHORN, R. A., GRAHAM, B. F., and GOODMAN, A. J. (1948) Standardised pain stimulation as controlled stress in physiological studies of psychoneurosis. *Science*, **108**, 509–11.

MANDLER, G. and KREMEN, I. (1958) Autonomic feedback: a correlational study, *J. Pers.*, **26**, 388–99.

MANDLER, G., MANDLER, J. M., and UVILLER, E. T. (1958) Autonomic feedback—the perception of autonomic activity, *J. abnor. soc. Psychol.*, **56**, 367–373.

MARAÑON, G. (1924) Contribution à l'étude de l'action émotive de l'adrénaline, *Rev. fr. Endocrinol.*, **5**, 301–25.

MAREY, E. J. (1868) *Du mouvement dans les fonctions de la vie*, Paris.

MARSDEN, C. W. (1971) Propranolol in neurocirculatory asthenia and anxiety, *Postgrad. med. J.*, Supplement **47**, 100–3.

MARSDEN, C. D., FOLEY, T. H., OWEN, D. A. L., and MCALLISTER, R. G. (1967) Peripheral beta-adrenergic receptors concerned with tremor, *Clin. Sci.*, **33**, 53–65.

MARSDEN, C. D., GIMLETTE, T. M. D., MCALLISTER, R. G. OWEN, D. A. L., and MILLER, T. N. (1968) The effect of beta-adrenergic blockade on finger tremor

and Achilles reflex time in anxious and thyrotoxic patients, *Acta endocrinol.*, **57**, 353–62.

MARSDEN, C. D., MEADOWS, J. C., LANGE, G. W., and WATSON, R. S. (1967) Effect of deafferentation on human physiological tremor, *Lancet*, **ii**, 700–2.

MARSDEN, C. D., MEADOWS, J. C., LANGE, G. W., and WATSON, R. S. (1969a) Variations in human physiological finger tremor, with particular reference to changes with age, *Electroencephalog. clin. Neurophysiol.*, **27**, 169–78.

MARSDEN, C. D., MEADOWS, J. C., LANGE, G. W., and WATSON, R. S. (1969b) The relation between physiological tremor of the two hands in healthy subjects, *Electroencephalogr. clin. Neurophysiol.*, **27**, 179–85.

MARSDEN, C. D. and OWEN, D. A. L. (1967) Mechanisms underlying emotional variation in Parkinsonian tremor, *Neurology* (Minneapolis), **17**, 711–15.

MARSHALL, J. and WALSH, E. G. (1956) Physiological tremor, *J. Neurol. Neurosurg. Psychiatry*, **19**, 260–7.

MARTIN, B. (1961) The assessment of anxiety by physiological behavioural measures, *Psychol. Bull.*, **58**, 234–55.

MARTIN, I. (1967) In *Manual of Psychophysiological Methods*, ed. Venables, P. H. and Martin, I., Amsterdam.

MERLO, A. B. and IZQUIERDO, J. A. (1971) Effect of post-trial injection of beta-adrenergic blocking agents on a conditioned reflex in rats, *Psychopharmacologia*, **22**, 181–6.

MICHIE, W., HAMER-HODGES, D. W., PEGG, C. A. S., ORR, F. G. G., and BEWSHER, P. D. (1974) Beta-blockade and partial thyroidectomy for thyrotoxicosis, *Lancet*, **i**, 1009–11.

MILLER, N. E. (1951) Learnable drives and rewards, in S. S. Stevens (Ed.) *Handbook of Experimental Psychology*, New York.

MISCH, W. (1935) The syndrome of neurotic anxiety: the somatic and psychic components of its genesis and therapy, *J. ment. Sci.*, **81**, 389–414.

MORALES-AGUILERA, A. and VAUGHAN WILLIAMS, E. M. (1965) The effects on cardiac muscle of beta-receptor antagonists in relation to their activity as local anaesthetics, *Br. J. Pharmacol.*, **24**, 332–8.

MORAN, N. C. (1967) The development of beta-adrenergic blocking drugs: a retrospective and prospective evaluation, *Ann. N.Y. Acad. Sci.*, **139**, 649–61.

MORAN, N. C. and PERKINS, M. E. (1958) Adrenergic blockade of the mammalian heart by a dichloro analogue of isoproterenol, *J. Pharmacol.*, **124**, 223.

MORUZZI, G. and MAGOUN, H. W. (1949) Brain stem reticular formation and activation of the E.E.G., *Electroencephalogr. clin. Neurophysiol.*, **1**, 455–73.

MOWRER, H. O. (1950) *Learning theory and personality dynamics: selected papers*, New York.

MUNDY-CASTLE, A. C. and MCKIEVER, B. L. (1953) The psychophysiological significance of the galvanic skin response, *J. exp. Psychol.*, **46**, 15–24.

MURMANN, W., ALMIRANTE, L. and SACCANI-GUELFI, M. (1966) Central nervous system effects of four beta-adrenergic receptor blocking agents, *J. Pharm. Pharmacol.*, **18**, 317–18.

MURRAY, T. J. (1972) Treatment of essential tremor with propranolol, *Can. med. Assoc. J.*, **107**, 984–6.

NICKERSON, M. (1967) New developments in adrenergic blocking drugs, *Ann. N.Y. Acad. Sci.*, **139**, 571–9.

NILSSON, L. (1960) *Physiologic and Biochemic representation of some psychiatric variables*, Stockholm.

NISBETT, R. E. and SCHACHTER, S. (1966) Cognitive manipulation of pain, *J. exp. soc. Psychol.*, **2**, 227–36.

NOBLE, P. and LADER, M. (1971) The symptomatic correlates of the skin conductance changes in depression, *J. psychiatr. Res.*, **9**, 61–9.

NORDENFELT, I., PERSSON, S., and REDFORS, A. (1968) Effect of a new adrenergic beta-blocking agent, H 56–28, on nervous heart complaints, *Acta med. scand.*, **184**, 465–71.

NORRIS, H. (1971) The action of sedatives on brain-stem oculomotor systems in man, *Neuropharmacology*, **10**, 181–91.

NOWLIS, V. and NOWLIS, H. H. (1956) The description and analysis of mood, *Ann. N.Y. Acad. Sci.*, **65**, 343–55.

OWEN, D. A. L. and MARSDEN, C. D. (1965) Effects of adrenergic beta-blockade on Parkinsonian tremor, *Lancet*, **ii**, 1259–62.

PAKKENBERG, H. (1972) Propranolol in essential tremor, Lancet, **i**, 633.

PAPEZ, J. W. (1937) A proposed mechanism of emotion, *Arch. Neurol. Psychiatry*, **38**, 725–43.

PARSONS, V. and JEWITT D. (1967) Beta-adrenergic blockade in the management of acute thyrotoxic crisis, tachycardia and arrhythmias, *Postgrad. med. J.*, **43**, 756–62.

PATERSON, J. W., CONOLLY, M. E., DOLLERY, C. T., HAYES, A., and COOPER, R. G. (1970) Absorption, distribution, metabolism, and excretion of propranolol in man, *Pharmacol. clin.*, **2**, 127–13.

PATON, W. D. M. (1961) A theory of drug action based on the rate of drug-receptor combination, *Proc. roy. Soc. Lond.*, Part B, **154**, 21–69.

PILKINGTON, T. R. E., LOWE, R. D., ROBINSON, B. F., and TITTERINGTON, E. (1962) Effect of beta-adrenergic blockade on glucose and fatty acid mobilisation in man, *Lancet*, **2**, 316–17.

PITTS, F. N. and MCCLURE, J. N. (1967) Lactate metabolism in anxiety neurosis, *New Engl. J. Med.*, **277**, 1329–36.

POIRÉ, R., TASSINARI, C. A., REGIS, H., and GASTAUT, H. (1967) Effects of diazepam (Valium) on the responses evoked by light stimuli in man (lambda waves, occipital 'driving' and average visual evoked potentials), *Electroencephalogr. clin. Neurophysiol.*, **23**, 383–4.

POLLIN, W. and GOLDIN, S. (1961) The physiological and psychological effects of intravenously administered epinephrine and its metabolism in normal and schizophrenic men. 2: Psychiatric observations, *J. psychiatr. Res.*, **1**, 50–66.

POWELL, C. E. and SLATER, I. H. (1958) Blocking of inhibitory receptors by a dichloro analogue of isoproterenol, *J. Pharmacol. exp. Ther.*, **122**, 480–8.

PRICHARD, B. N. C. and GILLAM, P. M. S. (1969) Treatment of hypertension with propranolol, *Br. med. J.*, **1**, 7–16.

PRIDEAUX, E. (1921) Expression of emotion in cases of mental disorder as shown by the psychogalvanic reflex, *Br. J. Psychol.*, Medical Section, **2**, 23–46.

RAMSAY, I., GREER, S., and BAGLEY, C. (1973) Propranolol in neurotic and thyrotoxic anxiety, *Br. J. Psychiatry*, **122**, 555–60.

REDFEARN, J. W. T. (1957) Frequency analysis of physiological and neurotic tremors, *J. Neurol. Neurosurg. Psychiatry*, **20**, 302–13.

REGAN, P. F. and REILLY, J. (1958) Circulating epinephrine and norepinephrine in changing emotional states, *J. nerv. ment. Dis.*, **127**, 12–16.

RICHTER, D. (1940) The action of adrenaline in anxiety, *Proc. roy. Soc. Med.*, **33**, 615–18.

RICKELS, K., LIPMAN, R., and RAAB, E. (1966) Previous medication, duration of illness and placebo response, *J. of nerv. ment. Dis.*, **142**, 548–54.

RICKELS, K., WARD, C. H., and SCHUT, L. (1964) Different populations, different drug responses. A comparative study of two anti-depressants, each used in two different patient groups, *Am. J. med. Sci.*, **247**, 328–35.

ROBISON, G. A., BUTCHER, R. W., and SUTHERLAND, E. W. (1967) Adenyl cyclase as an adrenergic receptor, *Ann. N.Y. Acad. Sci.*, **139**, 703–23.

ROSENBLUM, H. H., HAHN, R. G., and LEVINE, S. A. (1933) Epinephrine: its effect on cardiac mechanism in experimental hyperthyroidism and hypothyroidism, *Arch. int. Med.*, **51**, 279–89.

ROYDS, R. B., COLTART, D. J., and LOCKHART, J. D. F. (1972) Pharmacologic studies of indoramin in man, *Clin. Pharmacol. Ther.*, **13**, 380–92.

SAINSBURY, P. and GIBSON, J. G. (1954) Symptoms of anxiety and tension and the accompanying physiological changes in the muscular system, *J. Neurol. Neurosurg. Psychiatry*, **17**, 216–24.

SATTERFIELD, J. H. (1965) Evoked cortical response enhancement and attention in man. A study of responses to auditory and shock stimuli, *Electroencephalogr. clin. Neurophysiol.*, **19**, 470–5.

SCALES, B. and COSGROVE, M. B. (1970) The metabolism and distribution of the selective adrenergic beta blocking agent, practolol, *J. Pharmacol. exp. Ther.*, **175**, 338–47.

SCHACHTER, S. and SINGER, J. (1962) Cognitive, social and physiological determinants of emotional state, *Psychol. Rev.*, **69**, 379–97.

SCHÄFER, E. A., CANNEY, H. E. L., and TUNSTALL, J. O. (1886) On the rhythm of muscular response to volitional impulses in man, *J. Physiol.*, **7**, 111–17.

SCHALLEK, W. and ZABRANSKY, F. (1966) Effects of psychotropic drugs on pressor responses to central and peripheral stimulation in cat, *Arch. int. Pharmacodyn. Ther.*, **166**, 126–31.

SCHILDKRAUT, J. J. (1965) The catecholamine hypothesis of affective disorders, *Am. J. Psychiatry*, **122**, 509–22

SCHWEITZER, P., PIVONKA, M., and GREGOROVA, J. (1968) The haemodynamic effects of beta-adrenergic blockade in patients with neurocirculatory asthenia, *Cardiologia*, **52**, 246–51.

SHAND, D. G., NUCKOLLS, E. M., and OATES, J. A. (1970) Plasma propranolol levels in adults: with observations in four children, *Clin. Pharmacol. Ther.*, **11**, 112–20.

SHANKS, R. G., HADDEN, D. R., LOWE, D. C., MCDEVITT, D. G., and MONTGOMERY, D. A. D. (1969) Controlled trial of propranolol in thyrotoxicosis, *Lancet*, **i**, 993–4.

SHERRINGTON, C. S. (1900) Experiments on the value of vascular and visceral factors for the genesis of emotion, *Proc. r. Soc. Lond.*, **66**, 390–403.

SIEGEL, S. (1956) *Non-parametric statistics for the Behavioural Sciences*, p. 229; New York.

SILVERMAN, A. J., COHEN, A. I., SHMAVONIAN, B. M., and KIRSHNER, N. (1961) Catecholamines in psychophysiologic studies, *Recent Adv. Biol. Psychiatry*, **3**, 104–18.

SINHA, J. N., SRIMAL, R. C., JAJU, B. P., and BHARGAVA, K. P. (1967) On the central muscle relaxant activity of D.C.I., nethalide and propranolol, *Arch. int. Pharmacodyn. Ther.*, **165**, 160–6.

SJAASTAD, O. and STENSRUD, P. (1972) Clinical trial of a beta-receptor blocking agent (LB 46) in migraine prophylaxis, *Acta neurol. scand.*, **48**, 124–8.

SLATER, E., BEARD, A. W., and GLITHERO, E. (1963) The schizophrenia-like psychoses of epilepsy, *Br. J. Psychiatry*, **109**, 95–150.

SMITH, P. and BENNET, A. M. H. (1958) Vanillic acid excretion during stress, *Nature*, **181**, 709.

SOLOMON, A. P. and FENTRESS, T. L. (1934) Galvanic skin reflex and blood pressure reactions in the psychoneuroses. *J. nerv. ment. Dis.*, **80**, 163–82.

SOMERVILLE, W., TAGGART, P. and CARRUTHERS, M. (1973) Cardiovascular responses in public speaking and their modification by oxprenolol, in *New Perspectives in Beta-blockade*, 275–86, Horsham.

SPENCE, K. W., FARBER, I. E., and TAYLOR, E. (1954) The relation of electric shock and anxiety to level of performance in eyelid conditioning, *J. exp. Psychol.*, **48**, 404–8.

SPENCE, K. W. (1964) Anxiety (drive) level of performance in eyelid conditioning, *Psychol. Bull.*, **61**, 129–39.

STEINER, M., LATZ, A., BLUM, I., ATSMON, A., and WIJSENBEEK, H. (1973) Propranolol versus chloropromazine in the treatment of psychoses associated with childbearing, *Psychiatr., Neurol., Neurochir.*, **76**, 421–6.

STEPHEN, S. A. (1966) Unwanted effects of propranolol, American *J. Cardiol.*, **18**, 463–8.

STERNBACH, R. A. (1960) Some relationships between various 'dimensions' of autonomic activity, *Psychosom. Med.* **22**, 430–4.

STONE, W. N., GLESER, G. C., and GOTTSCHALK, L. A. (1973) Anxiety and beta-adrenergic blockade, *Arch. gen. Psychiatry*, **29**, 620–2.

STRANG, R. R. (1965) Clinical trial with a beta-receptor antagonist in Parkinsonism, *J. Neurol. Neurosurg. Psychiatry*, **28**, 404–6.

SULKOWITCH, H. and ALTSCHULE, M. D. (1959) Urinary 'epinephrine' in patients with mental and emotional disorders, *Arch. gen. Psychiatry* **1**, 108–15.

SUZMAN, M. M. (1968) An evaluation of the effects of propranolol on the symptoms and electrocardiographic changes in patients with anxiety and the hyperventilation syndrome, *Ann. int. Med.*, **68**, 1194.

SUZMAN, M. M. (1971) The use of beta-adrenergic blockade with propranolol in anxiety states, *Postgrad. med. J.*, *suppl.* **47**, 104–8.

SVEDMYR, N., JACOBSSON, B., and MALMBERG, R. (1969) Effects of sotalol and propranolol administered orally in man, *Europ. J. Pharmacol.*, **8**, 79–82.

TAGGART, P. and CARRUTHERS, M. (1972) Suppression by oxprenolol of adrenergic response to stress, *Lancet*, **ii**, 256–8.

TAGGART, P., GIBBONS, D., and SOMERVILLE, W. (1969) Some effects of motor-car driving on the normal and abnormal heart, *Br. med. J.*, **4**, 130–4.

TAYLOR, J. A. (1953) A personality scale of manifest anxiety, *J. abnorm. soc. Psychol.*, **48**, 285–95.

THADANI, U., SHARMA, B., MEERAN, M. K., MAJID, P. A., WHITAKER, W., and TAYLOR, S. H. (1973) Comparison of adrenergic beta-receptor antagonists in angina pectoris, *Br. med. J.*, **1**, 138–142.

TOLSON, W. W., MASON, J. W., SACHAR, E. J., HAMBURG, D. A., HANDLON, J. H., and FISHMAN, R. R. (1965) Urinary catecholamine responses associated with hospital admission in normal human subjects, *J. psychosom. Res.*, **8**, 365–72.

TOMPKINS, E. H., STURGIS, C. C., and WEARN, J. T. (1919) Studies on epinephrine, 2, *Arch. int. Med.*, **24**, 269–84.

TUNNICLIFFE, H. E. (1961) *Lecture to undergraduates on temperature regulation*, University of Cambridge.

TURNER, P. (1971) The role of beta-receptor antagonists in hyperthyroidism, *Postgrad. med. J.*, suppl. **47**, 97–100.

TURNER, P., GRANVILLE-GROSSMAN, K. L., and SMART, J. V. (1965) Effect of adrenergic receptor blockade on the tachycardia of thyrotoxicosis and anxiety state, *Lancet*, **2**, 1316–18.

TURNER, P. and HEDGES, A. (1973) An investigation of the central effects of oxprenolol, in *New Perspectives in beta-blockade*, edited by Burley, D. M., Frier, J. H., Rondel, R. K., Taylor, S. H., 269–72, Horsham.

TUTTLE, W. W., JANNEY, C. D., WILKERSON, D., and IMIG, C. J. (1951). Effect of exercises of graded intensity on neuromuscular tremor as measured by strain gauge technique, *J. appl. Physiol.*, **3**, 732–5.

TYRER, P. (1972) Propranolol in alcohol addiction, *Lancet*, **ii**, 707.

TYRER, P. (1973) Relevance of bodily feelings in emotion, *Lancet*, **i**, 915–16.

TYRER, P. (1975) A reappraisal of the James–Lange theory of emotion (to be published).

TYRER, P. J. and BOND, A. (1974) Diurnal variation in physiological tremor, *Electroencephalogr. clin. Neurophysiol.*, **37**, 35–40.

TYRER, P. J. and LADER, M. H. (1973) Effects of beta-blockade with sotalol in chronic anxiety, *Clin. Pharmacol. Ther.*, **14**, 418–26.

TYRER, P. J. and LADER, M. H. (1974a) Response to Propranolol and Diazepam in Somatic and Psychic Anxiety, *Br. med. J.*, **2**, 14–16.

TYRER, P. J. and LADER, M. H. (1974b) Physiological and Psychological Effects of *DL*-Propranolol, *D*-Propranolol, and Diazepam in Induced Anxiety, *Br. J. clin. Pharmacol.* (in press).

TYRER, P. J. and LADER, M. H. (1974c) Tremor in Acute and Chronic Anxiety, *Arch. gen. Psychiatry*, **31**, 506–9.

ULETT, G. A., GLESER, G., WINOKUR, G., and LAWLER, A. (1953) The E.E.G. and reaction to phobic stimulation as an index of anxiety-proneness, *Electroencephalogr. clin. Neurophysiol.*, **5**, 23–32.

VALINS, S. (1970) In *Physiological correlates of emotion*, edited by P. Black, New York.

VALINS, S. and RAY, A. A. (1967) Cognitive effects of false heart-rate feedback, *J. Pers. soc. Psychol.*, **4**, 400–8.

VAN BUSKIRK, C. and FINK, R. A., (1962) Physiologic tremor. An experimental study, *Neurology* (Minneapolis), **12**, 361–70.

VAN DER KLEIJN, E. (1971) Pharmacokinetics of distribution and metabolism of ataractic drugs and an evaluation of the site of anti-anxiety activity, *Ann. N Y. Acad. Sci.*, **179**, 115–25.

VAN ROSSUM, J. M. (1966) The significance of dopamine-receptor blockade for the mechanism of action of neuroleptic drugs, *Arch. int. Pharmacodyn. Thér.*, **160**, 494.

VAS, C. J. (1966) Propranolol in parkinsonian tremor; *Lancet*, **i**, 182–3.

VAUGHAN WILLIAMS, E. M. (1966) Mode of action of beta-receptor antagonists on cardiac muscle, *Am. J. Cardiol.*, **18**, 399–405.

VAUGHAN WILLIAMS, E. M. (1967) Central nervous system effects of beta adrenergic blocking drugs, *Ann. N.Y. Acad. Sci.*, **139**, 808–14.

VOEGTLIN, W. L. (1964) Management of functional gastro-intestinal disorders with diazepam, *Appl. Ther.*, **6**, 801–5.

WALK, R. D. (1956) Self-ratings of fear in fear-evoking situations, *J. abn. soc. Psychol.*, **52**, 171–8.

WALTERS, A. J. and LADER, M. H. (1971) Hangover effects of hypnotics in man, *Nature*, **229**, 637–8.

WATSON, J. P., GAIND, R., and MARKS, I. M. (1971) Prolonged exposure: a rapid treatment for phobias, *Br. med. J.*, **1**, 13–15.

WEARN, J. T. and STURGIS, C. C. (1919) Studies on epinephrin 1. Effects of the injection of epinephrin in soldiers with 'irritable heart', *Arch. int. Med.*, **24**, 247–68.

WEBB, W. B. (1948) A motivational theory of emotions, *Psychol. Rev.*, **55**, 329–35.

WEBER, R. B. and REINMUTH, O. M. (1972) The treatment of migraine with propranolol, *Neurology* (Minneapolis), 22, 366–9.

WECHSLER, D. (1958) *The measurement of adult intelligence* 4th edition, Baltimore.

WENGER, M. A. (1948) Studies of autonomic balance in army and air forces personnel, *Compr. Psychol. Monographs*, **19**, No. 4.

WHEATLEY, D. (1969) Comparative effects of propranolol and chlordiazepoxide in anxiety states, *Br. J. Psychiatry*, **115**, 1411–12.

WILCOTT, R. C. (1963) Effects of high environmental temperature on sweating and skin resistance, *J. comp. physiol. Psychol.*, **56**, 778–82.

WILKINSON, R. T. (1967) Evoked response and reaction time, *Acta psychol* (Amsterdam), **27**, 235–45.

WILKINSON, R. T., MORLOCK, H. C., and WILLIAMS, H. L. (1966) Evoked cortical response during vigilance, *Psychonomic Sci.*, **4**, 221–2.

WINER, B. J. (1962) *Statistical principles in experimental design*, New York.

WYKES, P. (1968) The treatment of angina pectoris with coexistent migraine, *Practitioner*, **200**, 702–4.

ZACHARIAS, F. J., COWEN, K. J., PRESTT, J., VICKERS, J., and WALL, B. G. (1972) Propranolol in hypertension: a study of long-term therapy, 1964–1970, *Am. Heart J.*, **83**, 755–61.